Mischievous in Mendham

a

Collection of Childhood Memories

≈

by

Gregory *L. Smith*

Mischievous in Mendham

"Mischievous in Mendham" is about Greg, a young boy, and his pals, growing up in a small country town of Mendham, New Jersey in the late 40's and follows their escapades for several years. Their journey through childhood is filled with exciting adventures and discovery. Some think the three are junior scientists as they construct an X-ray machine, some think of them as the little rascals with all the trouble they get into, while others think of them as three goofballs.

Greg gets into hilarious trouble at Hilltop Church that will have you in stitches. His family becomes the laughing stock of Mendham after he makes his first pirate radio and broadcasts one of their family gatherings, and he has a near encounter with a spirit in the cemetery when cutting the lawn.

They're mischievous at times, especially mischief night, as the three kids elude angry neighbors and even the police chief. One adventure will keep you in suspense, as they seek to find the ghost or whatever resides in the old red barn.

Aunt Holly, a protagonist, who has a rough time liking little boys, especially young Greg, has several hysterical run-ins with Greg. Knowing how she feels about him, he likes to torment her at every chance he gets, resulting in often hilarious outcomes.

The book also journeys through adolescence at Mendham Borough Grammar School, when Greg notices girls transitioning from just classmates to attractive members of the opposite sex. He also finds himself secretly enamored with the beauty of his best friends' sister, Kirsten.

for

Jansje B. Smith and Walter L. Smith, my parents

Contents

Chapter 1

The Haunted Barn

Mendham Borough, NJ 1951

The legend of the haunted barn popped-up during one of our childhood meetings down in my basement kitchen. My buddies, Al and Sam, third graders, and I, a fourth grader, were discussing my family's spooky barn. Was it haunted by ghosts? Did someone have an untimely sudden death on the property, leaving their soul behind? Was there someone or something still hiding out in the red barn?

Before I go on with the story, let me describe our properties. My friends' property and mine included additional acreage previously belonging to a wealthy family. The estate consisted of a large two-story colonial located on East Main Street in Mendham and two smaller homes. The smaller homes were probably used for caretakers and farm helpers, years ago. There were also three large barns, a chicken coupe, and a large tool shed. When my parents sold the main house to my buddies' parents, we moved into one of the smaller homes and added on an addition for more living space.

Several years later, my family took down two of the unneeded barns, leaving the large two-story red barn on the property. Historically, the local lore of the property was that two of the barns were haunted. These were the ones my parents demolished before I was born in 1942. My parents became concerned when whatever haunted the former two barns, mysteriously began to haunt the remaining two-story red barn. The red barn had a rickety stairway inside to access the upper floor. That area, at one time, was used for storing hay to feed horses and farm animals. Under the stairway, were two wood panels, flush with the floor. When opened, they would allow access to the dug-out dirt cellar. Both of these panels were sealed shut with numerous rusty nails, making them difficult for anyone to open and go down there. It always spooked me whenever I walked past them. *Was someone buried down there?*

The barn had a presence within it, maybe someone from a past life. Perhaps a restless soul in need to do one last thing before being buried six feet deep. When you entered the barn alone, especially at night, you felt someone or something was watching you. When it made itself known, it appeared as a bone-chilling gust of air that seemed to come out of nowhere. It was there one moment, then gone the next, as it drifted slowly away. Unexplained eerie noises happened frequently as you stood quietly within the barn; creaking floorboards, squeaking doors hinges, something falling on the floor, or a ghostly sound, as if someone or something was moaning. My family avoided going near the barn at night.

The wood floor panels drew my attention like a magnet. My curiosity often tempted me to grab a hammer and crowbar to pry one open to take a peak. The doors reminded me of coffin lids, being just about the same size.

One morning, when I walked into the barn, something was stirring down deep under one of the panels, I couldn't tell which one. Frightened, I ran back to the house where Dad was building some shelves in our kitchen.

"Dad, I heard strange noises in the barn coming from under those two spooky panels, something's down there, and it's alive!"

"It's most likely a porcupine, skunk, or groundhog that burrowed its way under the barn."

"What's down there below those panels? The way they're nailed with all those old rusty nails, it must be something spooky, maybe even a vampire! Did you nail those panels shut?"

"Not me. The former owner told me it was a dirt cellar, dug out years ago. He mentioned to me, that there were hundreds of old bottles down there and the place was covered with cobwebs. He also warned me it was crawling with all sorts of spiders and even snakes—too dangerous for anyone to go down there."

8

"I'd love to take a look down there."

"Don't you get any bright ideas of prying those panels open," Dad, warned me.

"What was it used for?"

"They probably used it for a root cellar to age wine years ago. People used to bury their garbage, there was no public garbage collection. Someone probably thought it was a good place to dispose of glass containers and booze bottles. Barns like this one had an interesting history. Years ago, hoboes used them for shelter and warmth as they traveled on foot from town to town to get to distant places."

"Do hoboes still use the barn?"

"I doubt it," said Dad.

♆

When I got together with my two friends, we couldn't stop talking about the barn, curious to know what might be down there.

"Bad things always happen at midnight," Sam said.

"That must be a creepy place in the dark of night, especially at midnight," Al said.

"You would never get me to go near that place that late at night," I chimed in.

"How scary could it be? We should check the place out, at midnight. We need a plan. How does this sound? We'll sneak out before midnight and meet at the split rail fence by the barn. Then, the three of us will go into the barn and investigate to see if it's really haunted. Let's do it tonight!" Al insisted.

"We can't do it tonight! At midnight it will be Friday, Friday the thirteenth. That's an unlucky day," I said.

"If there're ghosts in there, you can be sure they'll make their presence known on the 13th," Sam said.

"So, we need to do it tonight. We'll all meet at the fence five minutes before midnight. Bring a flashlight, too," I said.

9

Our conversation continued the entire afternoon, in-depth discussions on ghoulish stuff. What did ghosts look like? Did they only come out around midnight? Where did they go during the day? Could they harm you? Could they snatch you up and take you somewhere to turn you into a ghost? After hours of such ghoulish talk, all of us were on edge.

As dinner time neared, Al and Sam went home, leaving me with my thoughts. *Do I really want to do this? I could call them on our private telephone line and tell them I'm not coming.* I was deep in thought when Mom called me for dinner. My parents were religious, so we always said grace before eating dinner. As my dad had finished saying grace, I quickly interjected, "Please watch over us tonight."

Mom blurted out, "What was that all about?"

Dad, being very perceptive asked, "Now, what nonsense do you and the Larson twins have planned for tonight?"

"Not a thing, Dad."

"I've heard that statement one too many times. Come clean and spill the beans."

"I'm telling you, Dad, we've got nothing planned."

We finished dinner, Dad and Mom went to watch something on our new Dumont, black and white, 10" TV. I went to my bedroom and turned on the radio to listen to *The Lone Ranger* on WOR, 710 on the dial. *Sergeant Preston of the Yukon* came on after *The Lone Ranger*—those were my two favorite programs. Whenever I listened to my radio programs, I always turned my bedroom light off, which made the programs seem more realistic, like I was right there with the Lone Ranger or Sergeant Preston.

The Lone Ranger story was half-way through when a panic attack hit me. I ran across the room and flicked the light on. My heart was beating like an outboard motor at full speed. My imagination was running wild, but stuck on one thought. *Do I really want to do this at midnight?* With the light on, my heart finally slowed down somewhat. *Do I really want to go on this mission tonight?*

I glanced over at Little Ben, my alarm clock. I was nervous as my imagination ran wild. *The Lone Ranger* program had finished and *Sergeant Preston of the Yukon* came on. I listened intently and tried to take my mind off our midnight mission. In a flash, Sergeant Preston signed off, "Until next time….." *Would there be another next time for me?*

I set Little Ben to go off at 11:45 and wrapped the clock in my sweater so my parents wouldn't hear it go off. I turned off my light and tried to fall asleep, but couldn't. Mom always told me to count sheep to make me fall asleep. I tried, but suddenly they appeared as devilish looking ghosts, looking straight at me.

I abruptly jumped out of bed and turned my light on.

Mom knocked on my door and said, "I was going to bed. I saw light coming from under your door. Are you, all right?"

"Yeah Mom, just having a hard time falling asleep!"

"Try counting sheep."

"Tried that—didn't work."

"Turn out the light, close your eyes, and try again—you'll fall asleep."

"Good night, Mom."

I turned off the light, jumped into bed, and pulled the covers over my head. *It's safe under here, no ghost sheep can get me,* I thought and finally fell asleep. The midnight adventure hadn't even started yet and my mind was running wild with the thoughts of ghosts. I was so nerved-up that when I glanced back at Little Ben, he looked like a small monster with his face glowing in the dark. It only seemed like a moment later, that Little Ben went off.

I got out of bed, got dressed, grabbed my flashlight, and quietly went out the back door. The overcast sky concealed any light from the moon and stars—making it pitch black outside. I flicked on my flashlight. The batteries must have been weak. The flashlight only gave a dull yellowish beam that lit my way to the rail fence, near the barn. With each step I took, my body shook with fear, and my brain kept telling me; *this is a very*

11

bad idea. As I neared the fence, I saw two shadows about my size, Al and Sam. Somehow reaching my buddies steadied my nerves a bit.

"Everyone ready?" Al asked.

We walked cautiously together to the barn's door. The door was very heavy and it slid open or closed on a metal track above it. It always squeaked as you moved the door one way or the other. We pushed the door slowly open, trying to avoid making any noise that would alert anyone or anything of our presence. We opened it just enough to slip through. The moment we entered the barn we smelled it, an overwhelming musty odor.

"Guys, do you smell that? I never smelled that during the day in here," I whispered.

"It smells like really old wet clothes," Sam whispered back.

"It smells bad, like something died in here," Al added.

"Should we check this floor first?" I whispered.

We scanned the room with our flashlights. Mine was sort of useless. Then we focused our lights on the two floor panels. We checked the stairway, no ghosts there. We moved through another doorway, out to another section where the backup generator and tool benches were located. We motioned our flashlights around the entire room—nothing, all safe. We continued to cautiously walk into another section of the barn, the farthest from our entry point. Al headed in first because he had the better flashlight, Sam was behind him, and I was at the end.

Suddenly something swooped down out of nowhere on top of my head and clawed into my hair.

"Help! Something's attacking me!" I shouted.

Al focused his flashlight on my head.

"It's a bat!" he said, in a raised voice.

"Get the damn thing off!"

"I can't with my bare hands, it's liable to bite me. They can carry Rabies."

"Give me your flashlight, Greg, I'll find some work gloves," Sam said, as he ran off to do that.

I tried to stay calm until he returned.

Quickly coming back, wearing gloves, Sam said, "Bend down, so I can grab it,"

I did.

"Good. Got it! It won't let go. I'm going to have to pull it off, ready?"

He yanked hard and freed the bat from my hair.

It hurt like hell. "Am I bleeding?"

"Don't see any blood, but you may have lost some hair," Al said.

"What am I going to do with this thing?" Sam asked, as the bat flapped its wings wildly, trying to escape.

"Step on it and kill it," Al replied.

CRUNCH

"If there're any ghosts in this place, they'll sure know we're here with all our noise," I said.

We stood in silence and carefully listened.

CREAK!

"What the hell was that?" Sam asked.

"Just barn noise in the wind. Be quiet and listen."

Creek....creek....creek....creek.

We heard the noise coming from the second floor. We all stared at one another.

"Footsteps," I said.

They sounded as if they were coming from near the stairway.

13

"We can't use the way we came in. Whatever it is, it's over there," I said.

"We're trapped," Sam whispered, looking nervous.

"Nothing's going to scare me, I'll go back and check it out," Al said, as he started walking back toward where we had entered, leaving Sam and me standing there with the dim flashlight. He stopped at the doorway for only a moment, turned and ran back to us. "I chickened out! It's there! On the stairway!" warned Al with a look of horror on his face.

"What did you see?" Sam and I asked.

"Whatever it was, it started to come down the stairway. It looked really old, wearing ragged clothes. And it smelled like it just came out of a grave. Let's get the hell out of here!"

"Quick, follow me, I know a small side door that exits out into an open shed," I whispered.

In seconds we were out the small door. A large pile of boards blocked our way. We climbed over them, ready to jump down, when Al spotted it first—a skunk. It stood there staring at us momentarily and then ran away. Al and Sam sped off to their home and I ran for mine. My flashlight was so dim that it didn't help light my way. Occasionally, I glanced back to see if someone or something was racing behind to catch me. My light finally went out. I was going to toss it but decided it would make a good club. My heart pounded against my chest as I continued running in the dark. My legs were starting to give out when I finally saw the back door in sight. Exhausted, moments later, I ran up the back steps and through the back door, closed it shut, and slid the lock bolt home.

I stood there, leaning against the door, trying to catch my breath. Shaking, I risked a glance out one of the windows to see if it was out there, coming for me from across the dark backyard. Satisfied there was nothing coming for me, I headed to my room. Entering my room, I was never happier in my life to crawl back into my bed and hide beneath the covers, nervously waiting for morning to come.

Chapter 2

Gizmos

Mendham Borough, NJ 1949

Back when I was a kid, Mendham didn't have a supermarket. My parents had to travel to Morristown to do their food shopping. We did our shopping on Fridays, that's when Dad came home early from work. He worked in industrial sales, working countless hours other days and took Friday as a half day. Dad was the only one who drove. We used to have two cars. Dad got a big bonus one year and bought two Mercury sedans—his and her cars. On the first day, Mom had two accidents with hers, she said she had a perception problem. She cracked-up two front fenders in two separate accidents on the same day. She was able to get a new pre-painted black fender bolted on that morning after the first accident, to keep it a secret from my Dad. Then going home, got in a second accident—the same fender. After explaining her perception problem to my dad, she gave-up driving forever.

We shopped at the A&P store on South Street in Morristown, parking in the small lot behind the store. This was a weekly family event. Since I was the only one who ate cereal, I picked it out, and Mom shopped for everything else. I was always the first to reach the store's back entrance and headed for the cereal aisle. When we got to the cereal aisle, they told me I always took too much time deciding which cereal to buy. What they never realized, I wasn't choosing the best tasting cereal, but what gizmo was inside the box.

Before my parents even found a shopping cart, I had reached the cereal aisle. There they were, row upon row; Wheaties, Shredded Wheat, Kellogg's Pep, and many others. I couldn't read very well, so I just looked at the box for what was inside—not the cereal. The cereal companies liked to fool us kids. They made the toys look big, but when you looked inside the box, they were disappointingly tiny. Sometimes they made you collect box tops and send away for your prize.

Then you had to wait forever to get it. Most of the toys were made of plastic, except for the small metal license plates. They had one for each of the 48 states, Alaska and Hawaii had not become a state yet—a lot of cereal.

Going down the aisle I checked out the boxes for gizmos, A *Dragnet* whistle, a button of Popeye, Olive or other goofy comics, a US Navy Frogman pen that glowed in the dark, and a 6X microscope. I walked back and forth, trying to decide what prize I liked best. I narrowed it down to the frogman or microscope. After a few minutes, my decision was made—the microscope. I liked examining stuff, seeing how things worked. This would make everything six times bigger, even insects! They would be huge monsters! This toy was perfect!

By this time, Dad had picked up our meat and had joined my mom to do the rest of the shopping. I found them in the frozen orange juice section.

"What kind of cereal did you choose?" Mom asked.

"Shredded Wheat, supercharged with sugar, Mom!"

I held the front of the box against my chest hiding the microscope. Dad looked at me suspiciously. He always says he's got my number—whatever that means.

"I never knew you liked shredded wheat. It's kind of dry and coarse, like dead grass," Dad said.

"It's got to be good, Dad. It says it's sugar charged!"

"Remember, you chose it and you're going to eat it, all of it."

"Yup, every morsel, Dad."

"Put it in the cart," Mom said.

Still hugging the cereal, I said, "I'd rather carry it."

We got to the checkout counter; Mom placed our groceries on the counter while Dad was busy talking to the cashier. I set the cereal down, hiding the microscope as best I could. The cashier started adding up all the stuff. The belt inched forward, as he checked out each item with the cash register making a

16

ka-ching sound. I was holding my breath as he picked up my cereal. *Oh no! The 6X microscope picture is facing Mom and Dad.*

Dad stared at the box, then at me, "Remember, every morsel."

I nodded.

We got home and Mom started unpacking the groceries to put them away. I grabbed the cereal to take a better look at the microscope. All the way home, I kept adding to my list of things I wanted to examine. The temptation to use it was driving me crazy, I wanted to get it and hold it and start examining things. When my mom's back was turned, storing away groceries, I cautiously slid my finger under the flap to open the box. Unfortunately, Mom caught me, grabbed the box, and put it in the closet.

"Mom! I just want to see the microscope, just take a peek at it."

Dad walked into the kitchen, he heard me protesting about something and wanted to find out what it was all about.

"I caught him trying to open the box to get the prize," Mom said.

"We have to make a rule about cereal. I caught him the other morning with his entire arm down the cereal box, mangling it to pieces trying to get the prize out."

"Who cares Dad, I'm the one that has to eat it!"

"That's the problem, you get the prize, eat half the box and dump the rest in the garbage."

"I do not! I dumped it out on the lawn for the birds!

"Well, that's going to change. There's going to be a rule with cereal. No fishing inside for the prize. When it pours out of the box, you get it. No digging down in the cereal for it."

"Dad, you're making so many rules, I'm having trouble memorizing them."

Immediately, I started thinking of ways to get around this rule. Open the box from the bottom, push in the sides to make a round box, or dump out the entire box, get the prize, then pour it all back, that could work.

Saturday morning, I got up early. Dad was in the kitchen having eggs, bacon, and toast. I pulled out the shredded wheat cereal, grabbed the milk, a bowl, a spoon, and sat down across from him. He watched me out of the corner of his eye as I set the box down between us, with the microscope facing him.

"Remember, no hands in the box fishing for the prize," Dad reminded me.

"Yes, Dad, I remember." *Rule number twenty-seven.*

Dad put down his fork and watched me closely, like a person in the audience at a magic show watching how the magician did his trick.

Teasing Dad, I said, "Abracadabra." I flipped the box upside down, opened the flaps, pulled the waxed bag open, and slowly let a wad of shredded wheat drop into my bowl. Knowing that the prize was somewhere at the bottom, I shook the box several times until the microscope plopped out. To tell you the truth, the shredded wheat reminded me of a miniature hay bale.

"How long did it take you to figure that out?" Dad asked.

"Not long. As Mom always says, *where there's a will, there's a way.*"

Dad got up from the table to wash his dishes, turning now and then to look at me. I poured milk over my shredded wheat. It looked hard to eat so I broke it up into small chunks and took a spoonful—yuck! The cereal even tasted like dried hay, hay fed to horses. Dad didn't say a word, he just smiled as I chewed the hay to grind it up, just like horses do. *No wonder horses eat all day, it takes five minutes to eat a spoonful.*

He waited until I took a second spoonful. "Enjoying it?" Dad said. You only have about two more weeks of shredded wheat to go. Bye-the-way, your Aunt Holly is coming for

18

lunch today, so clean-up the kitchen after you're done—enjoy your cereal."

After Dad left the kitchen, I had to get rid of the awful stuff. There was a bathroom off the kitchen and I headed off to flush it down the toilet. I could hear Mom on her way to the kitchen. I didn't want her catching me in the act, flushing food down the toilet. She always says it's a sin to waste food because so many people in the world are starving. I didn't want her to hear the toilet flush, so I lifted the lid on the back of the toilet and dumped the cereal in the tank, then put the lid back. I just made it back to the kitchen when Mom arrived.

"Good morning, honey. Did you enjoy your new cereal?"

"It was okay."

Looking at the box which was upside down, Mom said, "I see you got your microscope."

"Yup, where there's a will, there's a way. Just as you told me, Mom."

"Aunt Holly is coming to join us for lunch today. So, don't you tease her or play some dirty trick on her."

"I won't, Mom."

I headed to my friends' house next door to play. When I got there, we decided to play war, fighting off the Germans using their parent's black Packard, pretending it was a tank. After several serious battles, we escaped without any injuries. We were on our way out of Germany when I heard my lunch bell clang. It was Mom's signal for me to come home.

Arriving at home, I opened the back door and walked into the kitchen. Everyone was sitting around the kitchen table, including my Aunt Holly. I ran over to give her a kiss on the cheek. She acted a little nervous when I kissed her. She always thinks I have a trick up my sleeve and that I'm a troubled kid. I heard her say that to Mom one day when they thought I wasn't around.

"Hi, Aunt Holly! Nice to see you!" I sat down at the table. Mom had placed a bowl of pea soup at each place setting. On the table, there were cold cuts, rolls, pickles, and other items.

19

Everyone was chatting away while they ate, especially Aunt Holly. She liked to talk, never stopped talking. According to Dad, she can go from one sentence to another without taking a breath. Sometimes she even gave me a splitting headache. We're half-way through lunch when Aunt Holly had to excuse herself to use the bathroom. I froze in my chair thinking about the toilet and what was sitting in the flush tank. *Oh crap!* A few minutes later, the toilet flushed. *I hope she doesn't look in the bowl.* I heard the second flush. A moment later, she opened the bathroom door, stood in the doorway, and looked white as a ghost. She looked so bad that I thought she was going to drop dead.

"I'm sorry, I need to leave. I'm not feeling well," she said.

Mom and Dad immediately got up from the table and walked over to her.

"I hope it's nothing you ate," Mom said.

"No Jan, but I better go home. If this bowel condition persists, I'm going to need to see a doctor."

I was having a hard time containing myself, ready to burst out laughing at any minute, but managed to say, without a grin on my face, "Sorry Aunt Holly, hope you feel better soon."

Getting back to the table, Dad and Mom conversed back and forth, about Aunt Holly getting sick. They were really concerned over her sudden illness.

"Getting sick so fast, it must have been something she ate. You didn't leave the mayonnaise out, did you?" Dad asked.

"No, of course not. We're all okay."

Mom set-down her soup spoon and stared at me. "Did you put something from your chemistry set into her soup?"

"Mom! I didn't do anything!"

Chapter 3

A Sip and a Tip

Mendham Borough, NJ 1949

The 4th of July came, and my parents had a party planned weeks in advance; the food, the soda, and beer. They also had planned several games; badminton, horseshoes, and croquette. They came up with activities for the kids, too; pin the tail on the donkey, skip rope, and board games. I asked them to have water balloons, too, but Dad gave his pat answer.

"We'll see."

I had accompanied my father that morning for the trip to Morristown to buy ice, cases of soda, and a keg of beer. I helped Dad pick out the soda and then we were off to the icehouse. When the guy came out the door carrying the ice block, I shouted, "Dad! That's the biggest ice cube I've ever seen!"

After several more blocks were loaded, Dad said, "That will keep the car cool going home."

When we got to the liquor store, my father said, "You have to stay in the car, children aren't allowed inside."

Why don't they allow kids inside? They probably think we might open a bottle and take a sip when they weren't looking.

A few minutes later, a big guy with a hand truck brought out a keg of Ballantine beer. I couldn't believe my eyes, as I ran out of the car to get a closer look, placing my hands all over the ice-cold container.

"Yikes! That's a beer can made for giants, Dad."

"You could say that, but the adults will really enjoy it."

The guy, with muscles like Popeye, lifted it into the back of our Chevy wagon and wedged it between the ice blocks.

When we arrived back in Mendham, I watched as Dad and Bert, my brother-in-law, unloaded the station wagon.

21

They removed the heavy ice blocks using giant metal tongs, placing them on the canvas sheet near the metal beverage tubs.

"You grab one end and I'll grab the other," said my dad. They moved the heavy beer can and placed it into one of the tubs. In one last trip, they carried out the wooden crates of soda for the kids.

Bert began working on the ice, chopped it into smaller chunks using an ice pick. Chunks broke off and scattered all over the canvas sheet.

"Bert, do you want any help?"

"Sure, you can put the pieces into the bucket, then dump them into the tubs."

"Boy, this stuff is really cold!" I said, holding a big chunk of ice in my hand. After I had filled the soda tub with several buckets of ice, my hands were freezing. They were so cold, that I couldn't feel my fingers. *They feel like they do when I make snowballs. I should have worn my mittens.* I slid my hands into my pockets to warm them up. After warming up, I collected more ice to pack around the giant beer can.

"This sure is a huge can of beer."

"It's really called a keg," Bert replied.

I followed Dad and Bert around the yard, setting up the games. They used a long tape to measure where to drive-in the rods for horseshoes, boundaries for the badminton set, and locating the croquette loops, and posts. I was bored and asked what I could do to help.

"Fill the grills with charcoal and put firewood into the fire pit," Dad said.

I took care of the grills and then began placing branches in a neat circle, just like the Indians used to do, arranging them so they pointed skyward as they leaned against one another in the center of the fire pit.

I spotted Aunt Holly's car pulling into the parking spot next to our house. It was a parking spot that allowed her an easy exit in case she suddenly wanted to leave the party without asking people to move their cars. In other words, a quick get-away if the kids were driving her nuts, especially me. She got out of her car and opened the trunk to remove food for the party.

"Hi, Aunt Holly!" I said, with smiling, while giving her a big hug.

She hugged me back and said, "Have you been a good boy?"

"Sometimes. I've got great news for you, Aunt Holly. Tonight, there will be fireworks. My brother, Walter is bringing sparklers, too. Dad said this year I can use some if someone supervises me. I'll get a few for you, too. And now for the super great news—we have water balloons this year!"

"Keep those away from me, I'm wearing a brand-new outfit today."

"I'll try. Need any help getting food out of the car?"

"Your hands look pretty dirty. Not a good idea for you to be handling things we're going to eat."

There she goes again. She thinks little boys are always stinky and filthy with dirt, especially me. She always says to mom that little girls are so much nicer, always clean and well behaved.

"Okay, have fun at the party, Aunt Holly. Maybe we could play croquette later, I'm not very good a throwing water balloons, but getting pretty good at driving a croquette ball."

Aunt Holly grabbed the large bowl of potato salad from the cooler in her trunk and shook her head looking at my filthy hands, as she proceeded to the house.

More cars arrived, filling the driveway; others that followed parked on the lawns wherever they found a space.

In the backyard, hot dogs and hamburgers sizzled on the grill, giving off a wonderful aroma. After greeting one another, partygoers grabbed one of the dozens of glass mugs on a table, got their drink, and headed for the grill. After getting their food, they sat down and chatted away.

Later in the afternoon, the adults began playing horseshoes and croquette. They liked to play in teams, to challenge one another. After the adults enjoyed a few mugs of beer, the party got louder, especially when someone scored a ringer or a player's croquette ball touched the finish pole.

I was really thirsty after helping Dad set-up for the party and headed for the soda. Sitting in the shade was my Uncle Nick.

In a Dutch accent, he said, "What a big boy you're getting to be."

"Dad says I'm growing like a weed; he makes a pencil mark on the kitchen doorway to show me how much I've grown. What's that yellow stuff taste like in your glass?"

"Kind of bitter, but good," as he patted his big beer belly. "On a hot day like this, it really hits the spot."

"Can I try a taste?"

"Sure, a little beer won't hurt you, but just a sip now."

He handed me the mug. With both hands, I tipped the glass eagerly to my lips. What was meant to be a sip, turned out to be more than a mouthful, with some dripping down and soaking my shirt.

He quickly took the glass away and said, "That's more than a sip, you're going to smell like a beer factory."

"You're right, Uncle Nick, it tastes bitter."

"You have to acquire a taste for it over time."

"How do you do that?"

"After you drink it a number of times it tastes better and better."

"Thanks for the sip and the tip, Uncle Nick."

On my way to get a soda, I saw an abandoned mug with a few sips left on the bottom. Making sure no one was looking, I drank it. *Still bitter. The more you drink it, the better it tastes.*

There're glasses all over with a few sips in the bottom. Still thirsty, I went for the next glass, and then the next.

On the croquette court, I saw Aunt Holly team-up with Aunt Aletta, seeking more people to play against them. I ran over to them, grabbed a red croquette ball and said, "The Smith brothers are going to challenge you. Walter, come on over here and be my partner. We're going to play our aunts."

My Aunts looked at one another with frowns on their faces as Walter, my brother, picked up a green ball and joined the game.

The game started out well, with everyone going through the loops until all four balls were clustered near the fourth loop from the finish line. Aunt Holly was playing to win, she had her ball all lined-up, a clear shot for the fourth loop, then my turn came up. She looked at me with a don't you dare look, as I glanced back at her with a devilish smirk on my face. With my body charged up from beer, I went to get a better look at the balls, took a step and fell down on my butt. *I feel dizzy and thirsty, I better get something to drink.*

"Time-out! I got to get something to drink," I shouted. "Be back in a second!" I ran to get a soda when I saw the full glass of beer sitting by the keg on the ground. *Can't let that go to waste. It tastes better the more you drink it.* I was so thirsty, I gulped it quickly.

Whatever was in the beer made me feel like 'super kid,' ready for any challenge. I was going to show those adults how I could do anything, even win our game. I arrived back at the croquette area walking back and forth looking at the scattered balls, trying to find a clear shot. Aunt Holly was fiddling around with her mallet, wondering what I was going to do.

"Would you take your shot, you're holding up the game," she said, with an impatient voice.

"Okay! Okay! Here come's my surprise shot. Watch this, Aunt Holly."

I wasn't looking at the next loop, but at her yellow ball. With my mallet poised, I tapped my red ball toward hers.

She gave me a dirty look, as my ball gently rolled over the grass and landed against hers.

"You missed the loop!" she said, laughing along with Aunt Aletta.

"Wasn't going for the loop," I said.

Walter said, "You're not planning to drive her ball out of the yard, are you? After all, she's your aunty."

Feeling confident, I placed my foot on top of my red ball, to secure it, and smacked it hard. Aunt Holly's yellow ball took-off sailing across the yard into the muddy dirt, the area where the pigs used to muck-in, near the red barn.

I broke out laughing, laughing so much that I nearly fell down again. I slapped my knees and said, "That's where all the pigs used to poop, Aunt Holly!"

Aunt Holly threw her mallet down on the ground, turned and looked at me straight in the eyes as she repeatedly jabbed her finger into her chest, yelling, "I was all lined up for the next loop! I was going to be the winner!"

"You were, but you forgot, you're playing against the Smith brothers," teased Walter.

Aunt Holly walked away mumbling, "Dirty little boy. Just a dirty little boy. His brother is just as bad. And to think, he's the town's police chief!"

We won the game, Walter came in first place and me in second.

I had to celebrate our win with a few more sips of beer. Shortly after, I ran around telling everyone how we beat the pants off both of my aunts. "They didn't have a chance against the Smith brothers," When I got to tell my Uncle Nick, he grabbed me by the arm and lifted me up on his lap. With a jovial laugh, he said, "Sometimes you got to play dirty to win! You played one heck of a game for a little fellow."

"Thanks, Uncle Nick. Can I have another sip of beer? Remember what you told me, each sip it tastes better and better?"

"You'll have to wait until next year. Besides, you reek of beer. Your mother is going to be really upset with me."

"Don't worry Uncle Nick, it will be our little secret."

I jumped down from his lap to look for another forgotten beer glass when I saw Aunt Holly standing in front of her chair. She was talking to my mother, complaining to her about how I played dirty, causing her to lose the game. Then she became angry and said, *"Jan, your son has it in for me. He drove my ball into the muddy pig poop area!"*

My mother broke out laughing. "Oh, come on, he's just a kid having some fun—give him a break."

"That's not all, I still think he put something in my pea soup at that luncheon you invited me to. I had diarrhea for two days! I know he was behind my getting sick, I just know it."

So I play dirty and poison the pea soup, Aunt Holly—time to get even with tattle tale Aunt Holly.

As she continued to complain about my behavior to mom, I went to the huge cardboard box that had the filled water balloons. I picked the biggest, a green one, which matched her chair seat that she was ready to sit down in. I carried it behind my back over to her chair. I pretended to drop something, and slipped it on her chair, walked away, and hid behind a tree near the soda.

Moments later, I heard a dull pop, her scream, and the loud laughter of people standing near her.

"My brand-new outfit! Where is he? If his parents wouldn't spank him, I will!"

"I heard my brother tease her, "You look pretty silly, Holly. You know we have bathrooms inside."

I was now feeling dizzy, and sick to my stomach, I went to get some ginger ale to sip. Mom always gives me that when I'm sick. I kept a low profile as I headed for the red barn, feeling like a spinning top, struggling with each step. I almost got there when a stream of yellow liquid shot out of my mouth like a firehose. I then fell to the ground, and that's all I remember.

It was sometime later after Aunt Holly had left the party wrapped in a towel around her butt, in a furious huff, that my mother asked other partygoers, "Has anyone seen Greg?"

Karen, a neighbor replied, "I saw him heading over to the red barn some time ago."

My mother had headed toward the barn calling my name when she spotted me laying down in the grass. She ran calling my name, but I didn't move. At the top of her lungs, she screamed, "Someone call the First-Aid Department—Greg's unconscious!"

Bill, a neighbor and member of the First-Aid squad, came running. He checked for a pulse, "Sixty-beat-per-minute—that's normal."

The games stopped as everyone ran to see what had happened to me. Some partygoers stood near me and yelled out their diagnosis.

"Probably has sunstroke," one said.

Looking at vomit around me, another said, "It's got to be food poisoning!"

My father had run off to call Dr. Hoffman on his emergency telephone number.

"Dr. Hoffman, speaking."

He's on the ground unconscious," my father said.

"Bring him to my office."

For two blocks, my father carried me, limp in his arms with my arms and legs dangling in the air.

"Bring Greg into my examining room," Dr. Hoffman said.

He checked my pulse rate, then placed his stethoscope several places on my chest as he intently listened to my heart.

My mother asked, "Is he going to be okay?"

"Dad added, "Are you going to call an ambulance to take Greg to the hospital?"

The doctor brought his index finger up near his lips. "Shhh." After listening around my heart, he said, "His heart's fine."

Dr. Hoffman started a neurological exam, lifting each of my eyelids and shining the small flashlight back and forth.

"His pupils are reactive."

The doctor smelled a strange but familiar odor and took a second whiff. He then straightened up and turned around to face my parents with his diagnosis.

"Well, this is a first, in all my years of medical practice— your seven-year old's drunk! Greg reeks of beer. Did you have the beer out where he could have consumed it?"

"We're having a 4th of July party today and have a keg on ice—he couldn't have gotten into that," Mom replied.

"Greg probably drank some mugs of beer left on the lawn," Dad suggested.

Just then I woke up, the room was spinning like a top, I didn't know where I was, except that Mom and Dad were there, along with Dr. Hoffman. Feeling awful, I threw-up all over the table and unfortunately, on the doctor."

"I'm sorry," Mom said.

"That's alright, it happens now and then, I'll take care of it. I think you hit the nail on the head folks; he drained a few glasses. I don't think it's necessary to bring him to the ER to pump his stomach. Just put Greg to bed and keep an eye on him. Kind of early in his life to be a drunk!" Dr. Hoffman kiddingly said with a grin on his face.

That's the last time I had a beer until later in life. Even as a senior at Morristown High School, when kids went to New York State to drink beer, I had absolutely no interest in joining them for the yellow stuff.

Chapter 4

Cub Scouts

Mendham Borough, NJ 1950

Scouting was very popular back when my pals and I were growing-up in Mendham. Mrs. Larson, the twin's mom, volunteered to be our den mother. She was a wonderful leader; she had the patience of a saint, to deal with our pack of nine energetic kids. We all met weekly at the Larson's house, down in the basement. It was kind of spooky, but with all of us scouts and Mrs. Larson, it proved to be a safe place to meet. The basement was not like most kids have today, finished with wallboard, wall to wall carpeting on the floor, and high-tech recessed lighting. This home may have dated back to the late 1800's incorporating architecture of that time period. The foundation consisted of large rocks stacked on top of one another and then cemented in place. Huge timber beams shaped by hand-tools, held-up the huge two-story center-hall colonial. The cellar floor was cement with several large cracks that developed over the years. The 'big house,' as it was referred to, was old and carried a long history over its residency, including an untimely death.

There was a big table in the basement that Mrs. Larson used for our pack meetings. Cub Scouts would meet on every Tuesday after school. We started our meeting saluting the flag with our right hands over our hearts saying the *Pledge of Allegiance*. This was followed by reciting the scout's oath. We each had a Cub Scout handbook that we brought with us each week. Mrs. Larson would go over each section with us, sometimes doing a demonstration. We had reached the chapter on first aid and Mrs. Larson, being a registered nurse, wanted us to get it right.

"First-aid is something that you will practice over your entire life, so this is important to remember. These are the steps you have to follow when giving first aid to an open wound.

First, you must cleanse the wound with soap and water, to get debris out," she said.

"Remember this the next time a drill slips and goes into your finger, Greg," Sam whispered in my ear.

"Everything has to be sterile—use a clean towel to dry the wound area. Next, apply iodine as an antiseptic. Does everyone know what iodine looks like?"

"It's red and stings like a bee sting," Andy chimed in.

With a box of band-aids in front of her, Mrs. Larson handed one to each scout. "We're all going to do this together. First you rip...."

(weeks later)

In April, we had nearly finished the book, we got near the end and got ready to close our meeting when Mrs. Larson suggested that we should celebrate our achievement with a dinner party for our parents.

"You kids are going to host it," she proudly said.

Al, Sam, and I looked at one another quizzically.

"Mom, what do you mean by that?" Al asked.

"That means, that this pack will be doing all the work. There will be cooks, servers, waiters, set-up and a lot of other little jobs. I'm going to make a list of jobs on a sheet of paper and each of you can sign your name next to one."

"Lets all sign-up to be cooks," Al suggested to Sam and me.

"Well, that sounds stupid, Al. None of us knows how to cook anything!" I said.

"We'll have to plan a menu for you to bring home to your parents," Mrs. Larson continued.

"Hot dogs, hamburgers, and baked beans?" Dick asked.

"No, something more elegant, something that will impress your parents—porcupine meatballs," she replied.

The kids exploded in laughter, several shouting, "Porcupine meatballs!"

Sam, whispered to his brother Al, "Tell Greg to get his 22-rifle ready to pop-off a few porcupines."

"With a sad look, Tom asked, "Do we have to kill porcupines for the meat?"

"Of course not," Mrs. Larson quickly responded.

"Just kill a cow," Bill whispered to Tom.

"It's the same meat your moms use at home for meatballs, except, we'll add white rice for quills. Since it's springtime, we're going to make strawberry barrel planters for your parents as a surprise gift to take home."

We all thought that was a really neat idea. The following week, nine empty nail barrels were lined up outside the twin's house. The scout pack spent the next two sessions marking-out and drilling large holes for the plants to stick-out. For the final touch, we painted them white. To keep them light in weight, we decided not to fill them with dirt, and leave the plants inside in a small container.

The next week we worked on our invitations, printing the what, when, where information. There was a big box of crayons on the table for scouts that wanted to be creative. Tom, still consumed with the idea of cooking a porcupine, attempted to color a plate full of food.

"Sam, standing next to Tom took one look at his invitation, "If your parents take one look at that plate of food, they're never going to come to our dinner celebration. Look at the length of those quills. No one in their right mind would eat that."

Tom looked at the plate of food he had just colored, concentrating on the quills and said, "Even a dog wouldn't eat those things," as he crunched the invitation in his hand.

As our afternoon meeting was coming to an end, most of us had completed our invitations. Some kids had to make several attempts to get the invitation presentable to take home. I thought I was done when Mrs. Larson came over and pointed to my spelling error—porkupine. Look at the sample, it's spelled porcupine, she said with a smile.

Al and Sam's mom checked each of our invitations and closed-out our meeting. It was a short walk home for me, living next door to my friends. Excited about the event, I ran with the paper and handed to my mom as she worked over the stove.

"Mom! Read this, it's really important! You and Dad are invited to a Cub Scout Dinner Party!"

As my mother read the invitation, she was smiling like she won a million bucks. "Lloyd, we're invited to a Cub Scout Dinner Party," to my dad sitting in the next room.

Dad, walked into the kitchen, somewhat less enthused than my mother, and read the invitation. He handed it back and said, "Of course, we'll come. What are porcupine meatballs?"

"That's a surprise. And guess who the chef is going to be?"

"Mrs. Larson?"

"Nope—Al. He's going to be the master chef, with Sam and me as helpers. We're in charge of making the porcupine meatballs!" I said with glee.

Fussy about food, Dad asked, "What's in the recipe?"

Teasing Dad, "A dead porcupine!"

"Count me out on that."

"Ground meat, onions, and rice. We have to make sure all those grains of rice are pointing out of the meatballs, so they look like miniature porcupines."

With a slightly sarcastic grin, Dad said, "I can't wait to try them."

The following Saturday, at the twin's home, nine busy Cub Scouts in their navy blue, gold trim uniforms scurried around the kitchen and dining room getting ready for the dinner party. We even wore our brimmed Cub Scout caps with the official insignia.

Mrs. Larson carried the work assignment sheet and assigned us our work assignments. She handed Al the recipe and told him where everything was in the kitchen. Sam and I followed Al into the kitchen to get started.

"Sam, you chop the onions—spare the fingers, please. Greg, you measure all the ingredients," Al said, as he fired up the stove to heat the large skillet. Sam began peeling the large onion, as tears quickly formed in his eyes. He took his arm to clear the tears as he began chopping the onion.

"This is an awful job you gave me Al!" Sam complained.

Looking at the big chunks, Al said, "Smaller Sam, pencil eraser size."

The chopping went on for some time. "Got the onion chopped," Sam announced.

"Dump everything in the mixing bowl guys," Al instructed.

Sam dumped in the onions, I dropped in the rice and the bread crumbs. As I read the recipe, the salt and pepper were specified using a small 't.' Looking in the kitchen drawer, I found a spoon with a capital T. I grabbed it and proceeded to measured out the salt and pepper. *What's the difference, a t is a T,* I thought?

"This pan is really hot. Both of you mix everything up as fast as you can," Al said.

"With what?" I asked.

"Your hands," Al replied, chuckling.

Sam and I hesitated. I don't know what was going through his mind, but yuck was going through mine. *Bloody meat*. Four little hands were squishing everything together when Al walked over and saw the measuring spoon with the 'T.'

"Who was the idiot that used a Tablespoon for a teaspoon."

I sheepishly raised my hand.

"Great! This ought to hit the pallet with one heck of a surprise," as Al held both hands on his head with the disaster at hand.

"Should we tell Mom?" Sam asked his brother.

"A little late now. There's nothing much she can do."

While Al walked out of the kitchen momentarily, Sam whispered, "They don't look at all like porcupines. I think we should add more rice on the outside of the meatballs. So, the two us opened the bag of rice and began applying more grains of rice on the outside of each meatball. We just got done in time before our fearless leader arrived back in the kitchen.

"Let's drop them in the pan, guys." As they dropped in the pan, Al commented, "Looks like you guys were a little heavy on the rice."

Our parents started arriving, with Mrs. Larson greeting each one at the door. "You're all in for a treat. Your sons prepared this wonderful meal all by themselves."

The three of us in the kitchen overheard her comment. We looked at one another with a worried look as we peered down in the pan of little balls of disaster.

Mrs. Larson, popped into the kitchen and asked, "Are you guys ready?"

"As ready as we will ever be," Al responded, as he transferred the little porcupines on a serving platter.

The servers arrived in the kitchen to carry out the garden salad, string beans, and Tom carried out the platter of porcupine meatballs.

"Don't drop them," Al warned.

The salad bowl was passed around the table first, followed by the bowl of green string beans. Tom, with a proud grin, held the platter of miniature porcupines for each dinner guest to help them self. We watched in horror from the doorway, waiting for someone to take the first bite. As luck would have it, it was my dad. We saw his eyeballs, almost pop-out of his head, as he sat there with a forkful of meat in his mouth not knowing what to do with it. With all the crispy sharp grains of rice, salt, and pepper, he was the first to swallow. He choked immediately, as his hand quickly reached for the glass of water to release the grain of rice caught somewhere in his throat.

The other parents fearing that may happen to them too, as they avoided the meat and began eating the string beans and salad. One by one, each parent braved the challenge to try our main entrée holding a glass in their other hand. Sam and I split for the kitchen ready to burst out laughing. Al followed with a pissed-off expression on his face.

"You know who is going to get the blame for this, don't you?"

"You are, the master chef," said Sam, with a grin on his face.

"Never again, never in a million years, will I ever cook with you guys!" Al retorted.

As our parents finished as much as they dared, the servers began collecting their plates. They arrived back in the kitchen with most of the little porcupines proudly still sitting on the plates, mostly, uneaten.

"I guess that was not a good menu choice," Mrs. Larson said, as we scraped the meatballs into the garbage.

She gathered us together and told us to bring in the planters from the garage. As we walked out the front door, our pack member grumbled back and forth on how we messed-up with the porcupine meatballs.

Al, grinned, patting Sam and me on the back and said to the guys, "It had to be a bad recipe."

A few minutes later, nine proud Cub Scouts carried their strawberry planters into the dining room to give them to their parents.

Still, to this day, every time I slip a fork into a meatball I remember our one and only scout dinner.

Chapter 5

Catholic for a Day

Mendham Borough, NJ 1951

Somehow the summer of 1951 passed too quickly. There were so many good times, summer vacation at the shore, swimming, and especially all the exciting electronic experiments my buddies and I did in our basement laboratory. Then there was our midnight adventure in the haunted red barn—we escaped the grasp of whatever hid there in the darkness of night or behind the many shadows inside. And here we were, back in school in September. Mrs. Carley was our fourth-grade teacher. She was a really wonderful teacher, friendly, kind, and patient. We had finished math, reading, and were studying chapter one in science. I didn't need to look at the big wall clock to see it was getting near lunchtime, the odor of fried fish had seeped up the stairway to the second floor from the cafeteria. The smell had crept its way under our door and filled our classroom.

Mrs. Waters was in charge of the cafeteria and prepared all the food for lunch, along with her two assistants. To accommodate children of the Catholic faith, Fridays were always meatless and today it was definitely fish—yuck! Fried fish was an unpopular menu choice with the kids, so most of us brought brown bag lunches from home.

Today, Friday, was not only meatless, but a day we also had a special class schedule. The last class period was either religious instruction at church or clubs & crafts. This was all new to me. This morning, neither Mom nor Dad, mentioned anything about a different class schedule. As the clock hands landed at two o'clock, the bell in the hallway clanged loudly. Mrs. Carley stood up and announced; "Kids going to church, line-up outside the classroom. Kids staying for clubs and crafts, stay seated." *Gee, where do I go? I don't have a clue. Since my parents are so damn religious, I better join the kids going to church. I don't want to start the new school year skipping church and getting in trouble with them.*

With that in mind, I got out of my chair, headed out the door, and patiently got in line. *Boy, this is really weird that Mom and Dad didn't mention anything about this.*

"Everyone follow me," announced Mrs. Carley. We followed her down the stairway, through the first-floor hall, and out the front door.

Kids from other classrooms joined us on the front lawn. The girls immediately segregated themselves and chatted away with one another with random bursts of laughter. The guys, we had a much different demeanor. Most of us were in a rotten mood, we'd rather be down on the ballfield playing a game of baseball. I was standing with Gary and Charlie, who was truly not happy about this.

Charlie looked at the ground as he kicked at the dirt and grass, and said, "This is bull shit! Who wants to be in church on a nice day like this. Maybe we can sneak out of line on our way to church and go to Joe's Luncheonette. I swiped a handful of change from my dad's pile of coins this morning. We can buy some bubble gum packs, the ones with pictures of baseball players inside. Maybe we might get lucky and end up with a Mickey Mantle card."

The last group of kids arrived on the front lawn as two mothers were tried to corral us in a group for the walk to church.

"May I have your attention!" Mrs. Esposito shouted. Everone ignored her and kept talking. "ONE MORE TIME! May I have your attention or do I get Mr. Latterlee out here!" Immediately, the kids stopped talking and looked at Mrs. Esposito. "Everyone line-up, we'll start walking to church— NO RUNNING!" Mrs. Esposito shouted.

"Yeah, right! Run to church, not a chance in hell of that," Charlie grumbled.

"I'm with you buddy," Gary added.

"I wish I could be home working on my new buggy," I said.

We walked down the center school walkway, past the flagpole to the public sidewalk, and turned right. It seemed to me that we should have turned left to go to my church, but Mrs. Esposito would certainly know the way to church.

We arrived at the center of town at the blinking traffic light and walked left on West Main Street. We continued on and there it was, a big white church building with a tall steeple. *This isn't my church! What am I going to do now? Maybe I should just sneak out of line and go home. If I get caught skipping school, that would be a first-degree punishment from Mr. Latterlee. I better just go inside. How bad could it be?*

"We should have split at the light for Joe's Luncheonette," Charlie said.

As we approached the church, we entered one of the two large white wooden doors and lined up to put some kind of liquid on our forehead. "What's that stuff kids are putting on their faces?" I asked Tom.

"It's Holy Water. Shhhh, you're not supposed to talk in church; you have to be respectful to God," he told me.

The line moved slowly ahead and my turn was coming up next. The kid in front of me did his thing and proceded forward to the center aisle. It was my turn. I stood there looking down at a bowl of Holy Water. *What happens if I touch this Holy Water if I'm not holy? I thought about all the bad things I had done all nine years of my life. Tricking my parents. Saying damn so many times. Stealing my mom's bra to make a double firing slingshot, as well as a list of other possible sins. Would my fingers fall off touching the water, being a sinner?*

Billy, standing behind me, nudged me with his elbow and whispered in my ear, "Would you hurry up; you're holding up the line."

I inched my fingertips into the bowl and swirled them around. *Feels like regular water to me.* I pulled my fingers out momentarily and carefully inspected them. *They looked okay to me. I better check my left hand, too.* I plunged my left hand into the bowl and pulled it out—my fingers were fine. *I guess I didn't sin that much!*

"Stop fiddling with the Holy Water," Billy softly said in my ear. "Don't forget to make the sign of the cross."

41

I was so mesmerized having survived the Holy Water test that I mistakenly thought Billy said for me to make a cross. I turned, looked at him, and whispered, "You got to be kidding. How am I going to do that? I don't have two sticks of wood, a hammer, and nails."

"Just make a cross with the Holy Water with your finger on your forehead, stupid."

Billy watched in horror as I took my left hand and made the sign of the cross—upside down.

"You got to use your right hand. You made the cross backward," he whispered.

I whispered back, "Should I do it again with my right hand?"

"You better. Remember, God is watching. Let me show you how it's done."

Billy zoomed through the motions as I tried to memorize what he had done.

I really screwed up royally. Here I am, a first-class sinner and I'm just a kid. Maybe God will give me one more chance to get this right.

Very embarrassed, with all the kids laughing behind me, I quickly took my right hand and made a proper cross.

Jerry, standing behind me, whispered, "Double crosser."

Oh my God! Can you imagine this sin on judgment day—a double-crosser?

Well, I waited for Billy to do his Holy Water thing. As I waited for him, I glanced at all the beautiful stone statues placed around the church. Over the sanctuary, there was a huge cross with Jesus hanging on it. *Didn't see a cross like that at my church.*

Billy walked in front of me and said, "Let's go." He took two steps on the red carpet, stopped cold, bent like he was going to kneel, but changed his mind and stood up. "What are you doing that for?"

42

"You've got to genuflect before you go down the aisle."

"If you say so." *Never did that at my church either.*

I tried to genuflect like Billy, but genuflected a little too much, causing my knee to land on the floor with a thud. Greatly embarrassed, I looked up and there were the three older ladies dressed in black with white head coverings, looking straight at me—they didn't look any too happy either. I got up and followed Billy and Tom into one of the church pews, along with other kids.

"We have to flip down the knee rest," whispered Tom. He quickly flipped the heavy board down before I got my legs out of the way. The board smacked my ankle on the way down— "Ow!" The priest and all the ladies in black turned around and gave me a stern look of disapproval. Everyone in our group got down on their knees and I did the same. While the kids prayed, I lowered my head in complete confusion on how I ended up at the wrong church. *Did I miss the group going to another church? What am I going to do now? If I split, the news will get back to that dreadful principal, Mr. Latterlee. If I stay here, I have no idea what to do. I'll make a fool out of myself and all the kids will laugh at me.*

When the priest brought out a small golden Holy Box from behind some red curtains, I really got nervous not knowing what would happen next. I quietly got up, looked down at the floor in hope that no one was looking at me, and headed for the front door.

Mrs. Esposito was sitting in the last pew and snagged me by my arm before I reached the door.

She whispered, "What are you doing here? You go to the Presbyterian church on the other side of town."

"I have no idea, Mrs. Esposito, I just followed all the kids."

"I'll walk you back to school," she said.

It was a ten-minute walk until we reached my school. She led me through the front door right to the office of Mr. William G. Latterlee, Principal. Mrs. Esposito sheepishly knocked on his open door—*she was scared of him, too!*

"We have a problem here, Mr. Latterlee. Greg went with the kids to the Catholic Church—he's Presbyterian." With his stern, scowling face, Mr. Latterlee looked at me through his thick round glasses and said, "He did? Well, we'll sort this out right now. Why were you going to the Catholic Church, Greg?"

"I just wanted to please my parents, Mr. Latterlee, make them proud of me. I chose to go to church rather than staying at school and having fun in one of the clubs."

Mr. Latterlee's scowl transitioned into a reserved smile as he chuckled to himself. "Well, Greg, the good news is that next Friday, you can have fun doing an activity or club; the bad news is that today, you have to keep me company until three-fifteen. Sit down here in the chair in front of my desk."

I sat straight up in the chair, like a military cadet, and watched Mr. Latterlee fill out papers and write notes in his black spiral book. *That's the book he probably keeps notes on kids, the bad ones. I wonder if he's writing about me.* Sweat poured down my face as I sat a few feet away from him. I had never been this close to him before. My eyes focused on his features, his balding head, big eyes that peered through his thick frameless glasses, and his chubby hand that held the fountain pen of doom. Many thoughts bounced around in my mind, but one prevailed. *In the blink of an eye, he could fail me or any other kid for the year.* I sat focused on that thought when the three-fifteen bell went off outside his office. "May I go now, Mr. Latterlee?"

"See you next week, Greg."

I headed home, got to my room, and got changed into my play clothes. Arriving at the kitchen to grab a glass of chocolate milk and a few cookies, there was Mom.

Mom asked, "How was your day at school?"

"Well Mom, I got to go to a Catholic Church today, the one on West Main Street.

"You did what? You're not Catholic!"

"How did that go?"

44

"I passed the Holy water test, but messed up making the sign of the cross using my wrong hand. I was so nervous with everyone watching me, I made the cross upside down and had to do it again with my right hand. One of the kids called me a double-crosser. God's not too happy with me right now I bet.

I also tried to genuflect like Billy but slammed my knee against the floor. The ladies in black and white turned and glared at me."

"I'm sure God has forgiven you," My mom said, smiling.

"What if he hasn't, Mom? I know I was only a Catholic for a day, but I wasn't a very good one."

"I'm sure God appreciated the effort. Don't you worry," my mom told me, making me feel a lot better. Each Sunday on my way to Hilltop Church, I pass the Mendham Roman Catholic Church and wonder what the ladies in black said about me that day. I'm sure Mr. Latterlee enjoyed telling the story about the boy who ended up in the wrong church.

Chapter 6

Buggies

Mendham Borough, NJ 1950—1952

Growing up in a small country town, during the fifties, in economically challenging times, was quite different from what kids experience today. We didn't have a lot of kid stuff to play with. Basically, some sporting equipment, a baseball and maybe a leather baseball glove, and some board games.

So, if you were lousy at sports, as I was, you had to find other things to do. My overwhelming interest was how things worked. My interest was pretty much divided between mechanical and electrical things. I read "*Popular Mechanics*" and "*Popular Electronics*" from cover to cover. Many of my days, when not in school, were spent building projects shown in those magazines. My practical experience came from taking apart almost anything I could get my hands on, which usually were lawnmowers, radios, and phonographs.

On my way home from grade school, I would stop at either Gunther Chevrolet or the Sinclair Gas Station, directly across the street from the dealership, to check-out their discarded auto parts. Greasy, oily parts were thrown in a pile behind both buildings. Curiosity always prevailed. I usually ended up carting home a horn, a steering wheel or some other interesting part.

Sometimes, I stopped at the Sinclair Station where they had several used Ford, Model T vehicles; trucks, coupes, and convertibles sitting outside in front of the station. A guy named Dewey worked there. He pumped gas, repaired cars, and drove the daily school bus between Mendham and Morristown High School. He was sort of heavy, in his thirties, good-natured, and always joked around. Kids really liked him. He was very tolerant of me. Often after school, when I walked into the gas station, I would ask if I could sit behind the wheel of one of the T's. What excitement for a kid, to look over the huge black hood, grab the steering wheel with one hand and the stick shift with the other, pretending to drive.

This encouraged me to build, what I called, a buggy, like a modern-day derby car, but not as fancy in design. Over several years, I made several refinements each time I built a new buggy. None of these were motorized. They were fabricated with parts that I had scrounged from around town. My buggies were made of disposed lumber from homes under construction. Wheels and axles came from disposed baby carriages. It must have made people curious seeing me pushing a baby carriage to my house. Back in the fifties, power tools were not contemporary tools at home. Hand saws, files, and hand drills were found hanging above most home workbenches.

Cutting a baby carriage steel axle to a shorter length was difficult, it took a great deal of time. I needed to use a hacksaw. Most often, the blade was dull, making it difficult to cut. It often left several blisters on my hand and a nicked finger or two. Drilling a small hole in the axle to secure each wheel with a bent nail or cotter pin was almost impossible. It often resulted in a drill bit suddenly breaking or drill slipping off the center on the round axle and going into my finger.

The basic buggy was built on a wood chassis, using a board about five feet long, a 2 by 8 or 2 by 10 dimensional piece of lumber. Two other pieces of wood would be used to hold both axels to the chassis.

A single loose bolt or screw was used in the front to secure the moveable steering axle. The back axle was held in place with several screws or nails. The seat was fabricated with additional boards to support my back at a comfortable angle. It was mounted at a position on the chassis so that my feet could operate the front steering bar.

As time went on, I added more refinements, such as a friction brake. This was just a simple wood lever that rubbed against one of the back wheels. It worked most of the time. If that failed, my emergency brake was my two feet jammed against the ground. To make my buggy more realistic, like a car, I added an empty nail barrel for the engine and hood. I even painted a make-believe engine on both sides of the barrel.

Months later, I wanted to add a Chevy steering wheel that was in my inventory of car parts. It would require a large wooden dowel. Not having the money for one, I sawed off the end of mom's broom handle. Mom was in for a surprise the next time she swept the kitchen floor. The steering wheel was attached at one end of the handle. The other end went through two holes drilled on an angle through the nail barrel. This iteration allowed my imagination to give me the illusion that I was driving a real car.

The following Sunday morning, while attending church with my parents, not paying any attention to what the minister was saying, I figured out how to make the steering wheel work. To do that, I needed to drill a hole through the center of the broomstick and thread a piece of rope through the hole and wind it with several turns clockwise on one side and counter-clockwise on the other. Each rope end would then go through a pully at a right angle to each side of the front axle.

I kept looking at the clock at the back of the church, wishing for the service to end. Inspired by the idea, I couldn't wait to get home and try it out. Dad's work area in the spooky red barn was a great resource for almost anything. He bought most things in bulk quantity. Sometimes, the storage shelves reminded me of a hardware store. Everything labeled and neatly stored in place. Odd stuff was destined for the marked empty coffee cans. Pulleys were not a common thing to have around in the workshop. But inside a can marked 'what not,' I found a pair.

After lunch, I ran to the barn to start my project. After I drilled the rope hole in the broom stick, I realized it was too big and weakened the steering shaft. Sunday was really a holy day back then, so all the stores and gas stations were closed. Only Robinsons Drug Store was open in town; you could only buy prescription drugs, but not an ice cream cone—the fountain counter was closed. Towns like Ocean Grove, chained their main roads off to prevent cars from entering. Sundays were devoted to going to church and visiting relatives, period.

Thank goodness Sunday restrictions didn't apply to me building stuff. So off I went to look for another broom. The kitchen broom was not a candidate. If I took off another chunk,

49

Mom would be down on her knees sweeping the kitchen floor. I looked and looked, none could be found. I either had to confiscate one of Dad's long-handled tools or confiscate Mom's new broom I found stored in the basement. Rather than deal with Dad's fit of lunacy over a missing tool handle, I grabbed Mom's broom from the basement.

This time, I checked the drill bit diameter before drilling. After successfully replacing the wood shaft with the correct size hole, I attached the rope and tested it out. Good news, bad news. It worked, but the front wheels only moved a small amount, not enough to fully steer. More turns of rope on the broomstick were required. With another longer piece of clothesline, I added more turns of rope and tested the steering again. It worked like a charm.

It was time to test drive the buggy. My yard was flat so I had to ask my buddies, Al and Sam to push me around the backyard. I felt like a race car driver as I steered the car around an imaginary race track. My buddies got tired of me driving and them pushing. The buggy came to an abrupt stop, until I said, "Let's take turns." We all took turns driving the buggy, but that got old, too. Then an idea hit me, why not use Dad's Bolens walk-behind tractor to pull the buggy? We ran the tractor for hours until it ran out of gas. Luckily, there was more gas in the barn.

One afternoon, while walking home from school, I suggested to Al and Sam that we take the buggy to the top of Orchard Street, not far from our homes. Orchard Street was about a quarter-mile downhill run to Gunther Motors that intersected with East Main Steet, now 1-24.

With a tow rope, we towed the buggy the one-quarter mile trip to the top of Orchard Street. At the top of the hill, I was ready to coast down the street.

Back then, it was safe to play in the street. Families only had one car for dads to go to work. Moms stayed home to raise the family. The only safety concern we had was that a mechanic might exit Guthers to test drive a repaired car and collide with the buggy.

"Are you ready, Greg?" Al asked.

50

"Yeah! Give me a running push." Both Al and Sam gave me one heck of a start. I zoomed down the road, whizzing by all the houses, gaining more speed every second. There was some play in the steering control that caused the buggy to veer one way, then the other. It must have looked as if a kid had gotten hold of his dad's beer. The buggy swerved back and forth, making it all the way down to Main street. As I approached the car dealership, the buggy slowed down.

Suddenly a mechanic came walking out of Gunther's to bring a car in for service. I nearly clipped him. As I drove by, he said, "I love that steering wheel."

After coming to a stop, I pulled the buggy back to the top of Orchard Street for my friends to give it a go. When I got there, I tightened the rope to fix the steering problem. After several rides down the hill, we were exhausted and headed back home. Just-in-time, too, as cars started to appear in town as dads were coming home.

Two weeks later, at one of our meetings, my friends and I decided to motorize the buggy. It was solely my idea to secretly remove the gas motor off one of my dad's lawnmowers. The easiest one was my father's favorite trim mower, an orange-colored, Jacobson. A real beauty, he kept it meticulously clean.

We had it all planned out. We'd wait for my dad to go on a business trip. So daily, as we ate our breakfast together, I would ask Dad, "Where are you off to today?" My dad was an industrial salesman for Sherwin-Williams. Finally, one day Dad said, "I've got a meeting out on Long Island today."

Bingo—this was the day.

I looked for my friends Al and Sam at school to tell them the good news. Today we're going to motorize the buggy. School seemed to drag on, hour by hour. Finally, the 3:15 buzzer went off. I sprinted out of school for home.

Once home, I changed my clothes and ran out of the house to the red barn. I pushed with all my might to slide the big door all the way open. This was to get as much light inside as possible, to keep the ghosts at bay. Unfortunately, the Jacobson

51

was stored near the spooky coffin lid panels on the floor. I cautiously walked to the machine, grabbed it by both handles, and pulled it out of the garage, then back to Dad's tool bench for various size wrenches.

Al and Sam arrived at the barn. We had lots of work to do. The engine needed to be removed, we needed to attach a pulley to the back axle, and secure the back wheels to the axle. The last part would be to add the drive belt and the gas engine. We split up the work to save time. I did the metal drilling, having had more hazardous duty experience.

Finally, we bolted the engine on. Sam had filled the tank with gas, I sat behind the wheel, and Al wrapped the pull cord around the starter. He was ready to give it a yank when we spotted my dad's green Chevy station wagon rapidly approaching us down the long driveway. Dad garaged his car in the haunted red barn every night. He suddenly stopped in front of the buggy. He immediately got out of his car and began to rant in a raised voice.

"What the hell do you think you're doing?"

"Nothing, Dad," my answer for anything questionable that I did.

"Don't give me that crap! I'll give you one half-hour to put the motor back on my Jacobson mower! When I come back, it better be on!" he shouted.

It was all hands on deck as we disassembled the engine from the buggy and place it onto the mower's deck.

"Anyone see the mower bolts?" I asked.

"No," said Sam.

Time had evaporated, we only had five minutes more to our deadline. "I'll look for some bolts from Dad's stash. We can just push them through the motor mounting holes and it will appear that it's mounted." I ran into the barn, past the coffin lids, to Dad's parts inventory, and grabbed four bolts. A minute later, I pushed them in place—lawnmower re-assembled.

We no sooner parked the mower by the coffin lids, when Dad appeared in the garage. Still looking really pissed, he continued shouting his litany of orders.

"You're never to touch that mower again! You're never to use my wrenches! You're driving me nuts. The minute my back is turned, you're taking something apart or getting in trouble. I'm going to use that mower this weekend."

Dad walked out of the barn. Just then, I heard Mom ringing the dinner bell. We slid the door closed, my friends went home and I headed to my house for dinner. On my way there, I kept thinking, *I better find those missing bolts and nuts. If Dad goes to start that engine, it will fall off the deck and land on his feet.*

Just before I got to the house, I felt something in my pocket. I reached in. The bolts. I ran back to the barn and put them in place as quickly as I could, but I was missing one. I hoped Dad wouldn't notice the missing bolt when he set out to cut the lawn because if he does, he'll take away my soldering iron and shut down my basement lab for who knows how long.

When I got to the kitchen, Mom had dinner on the table. Dad's blood pressure must have been really high, his face was beet red. I sat down and said nothing. My one pocket felt heavier than the other, *did I forget to put back a tool?* I slipped my hand inside my pocket—the missing bolt. Dad began saying grace. As he finished, I thought, *thank you, God, once again.*

Chapter 7

William G. Latterlee

&

The Wild Horses

Mendham Borough, NJ 1948-56

William G. Latterlee was our principal during my attendance at Mendham Borough Grammar School, now called Hilltop School. The school was a two-story red brick building located on Hilltop Road, with the school's office on the immediate left upon entering the building.

Mr. Latterlee was a man that teachers respected and kids feared. He was the scariest guy you ever saw; short, stocky, and wore special glasses that magnified his dreadful eyes. Those eyes never missed anything out of order, especially the kids. Everything got stored in his brain. He'd disseminate that information later, to solve mischievous acts done at the school. Most of his hair was gone, probably caused by his brain overheating, trying to come up with ways to punish trouble-making students.

At kindergarten and first grade, we had little or no interaction with Mr. Latterlee. That changed though in the upper grades.

During our school year, he spied on us, showing up when we least expected him. He would stand quietly outside our classroom, peeping through the small glass window at us. His eyes scanned the room, back and forth, row by row, looking for a kid screwing around. We always exhaled a breath of relief when his head disappeared from the doorway.

What was worse was when he monitored our class. He even checked out the teacher too, making sure the lesson was tough enough. Except for the teacher's voice, you could hear a pin drop in our classroom. We sat straight up, perfect posture in our chairs, listening to every word the teacher said.

We appeared to be model students. We played this game until we heard him get out of his chair and leave the classroom. Then the model students suddenly transformed into carefree country kids, slumping in their seats, no longer paying attention to the teacher.

He also made the announcements at our assemblies. I was in the audio-visual club and had to set-up the professional audio system on top of the stage, along with a microphone for him to use. I played a record containing Sousa Marches for the kids entering the auditorium—they never marched once.

As the kids poured into the auditorium, there was complete pandemonium. Guys pulled girls hair, smacked fellow students on the head, and shot spitballs at unsuspecting victims. Some students came prepared, bringing marbles from home. After his announcements, Mr. Latterlee exited the room. Then, the lights dimmed to almost total darkness, and the marbles began dropping to the floor. Clank, bang, clank, they would go, as they rolled down the floor, one by one, hitting the seat frames, row by row. Kids broke out in loud laughter. Above the din, a teacher would shout up to the second-floor projection booth, "Turn on the lights." The auditorium lights would come on, and teachers would grab the guilty for a visit with Mr. Latterlee.

Things got a lot worse in seventh grade when we got our new teacher, Mr. Lonzo. Periodically, some boys became unruly, showing off to the girls. Our teacher was very strict and had little patience. He also had a horrible temper. When he reached his boiling point, he exploded with fearful verbiage, slamming his textbook down on one a kid's desks in the front row. That's where all the studious students sat—all girls. The guys sitting in the back had another term for them—the brown-nosers or teacher's pets. The violent disciplinary rant echoed back and forth in the room. We were never prepared for one of his sudden explosions. We cringed in our chairs when he would start his rant, then slam his book on one of the desks— probably causing that student to wet their pants.

With his pointed finger, he'd scream, "Think you're a wise guy! Well, we'll see about that when Mr. Latterlee gets done with you. You're also staying after school for detention with me. Get down to the office—now!"

I only got sent to the office once for discipline; in my case, it was being in the wrong place at the wrong time. It happened by accident, but no one believed my story. They thought I had made it up—too crazy to be true.

To earn spending money, I trapped muskrat, raccoon, and mink along streams near my house. Mark, one of my classmates, also trapped. He set his traps on the other side of town.

Every morning, Little Ben, my alarm clock, went off at 6:00 a.m. I jumped out of bed, got dressed, downed some cereal, and woke Mark up—he didn't have an alarm clock. He lived two blocks away from me and slept in a second story bedroom. As a creative kid, he made his own alarm clock. It consisted of several cans tied together and attached to a long string that draped out his window for me to pull. It was my job to wake him up each morning. I yanked on the string until he woke up. To signal me that he was awake, he would yank the string from his end.

I would then set off to check my traps. These were located a mile away, down in a pasture, behind a large horse stable. A beautiful, fast running stream ran through the back pasture, a place where wild animals visited. To get to the stream, I had to climb over a high fence.

I had climbed the fence, checked my traps, and was heading back when I heard a loud rumble. Alarmed, I looked around to find where the noise was coming from. About two dozen galloping horses were heading for the stream and at me! It was winter and the cold air made the horses very spirited. Clouds of steam came from their nostrils as they approached. *I'm going to be trampled to death!* There was no time to reach the fence, it was just too far away. They were getting closer, and I had to do something.

Several trees were nearby, mostly birch, growing along the stream bed. A small, but tall, birch tree was the closest to me. My only chance of escaping severe injury or death was to climb it and climb it fast. Adrenaline poured through my veins as I shimmied up the tree, six inches at a time, to reach the first branch, ten feet from the ground. I barely reached the first branch when the horses arrived. I unwrapped my legs from around the tree and placed one foot on the branch. I hoped that it would be strong enough to support my weight. Two horses brushed themselves against the tree, causing it to sway back and forth. I held on for dear life. With my weight, the tree swung back and forth like a clock pendulum, making me dizzy. My heart pounded rapidly not knowing my fate.

They knew I was up in the tree, but I was not welcome in their territory. The stallions were protective of the herd and approached the tree snorting and squealing at me, a threat in their domain. They looked at me with their wild eyes and began to try to shake me out by ramming their bodies against it. I swung back and forth with my arms and legs tightly wrapped around the tree. There was no question about it, they wanted me out to trample me with their hooves. *This tree is not going to take much more of this. It's going to snap or fall down. Was the force of a fifteen-hundred-pound horse more than a tree could take?*

I didn't have a watch, but, I knew by the sun's position the eight o'clock school bell had rung a long time ago. *If I survive the horses' assault and get out of here, I'll be very late for school—an unexcused tardy absence.* The stallions continued slamming against the tree until they heard something.

Back at the barn, the farmer whistled for them to return. After they got a safe distance away, I slid down the tree, ripping my cotton gloves, pants, and cutting my hands. When my feet hit the dirt, I ran for the fence.

Knowing that I was very late for school, I ran and jogged most of the two-mile distance to school. After arriving, I slipped through the side door, out of breath. I had to avoid being seen by the office staff. I snuck up the grey metal stairs to my classroom on the second floor. The door was closed, I slowly opened it, slipped through, and got to my desk. I opened my math textbook and stared at the exponential problems scribbled on the blackboard.

"Greg! Why are you just getting here at nine-fifteen?" Mr. Lonzo asked in a raised voice.

"A bunch of horses chased me up a tree!" I don't think Mr. Lonzo was prepared for what he'd heard, an inventive answer. He stood speechless, while the class broke-out in hysteria.

"Alright, quiet everyone! Do you have a note from home?"

"NO! How was I supposed to do that, swinging back and forth in a tree for over an hour? I'm lucky to be alive!"

The class laughed again, even louder.

"Well, you go right down to Mr. Latterlee's office and explain that situation to him. Don't come back until you have a written pass from him either."

I got up out of my seat, sweating, heart racing, overwhelmed thinking about going to see Mr. Latterlee. Over the last seven years in school, I had never gotten into any trouble, and never got sent to the office, except for going to a Catholic Church when I was a Presbyterian. Slowly, I descended the stairs, walked down the hallway to the main office. I stepped up to the counter; the secretary was busy typing. She sensed my arrival, stopped typing and looked at me.

"May I help you?"

"Mr. Lonzo sent me down to see Mr. Latterlee."

"Well, that's not good news, Greg. Sit in the chair against the wall and I'll ring him." His telephone rang three times. "Mr. Lonzo has sent a student down to see you. It's Greg Smith. Okay, Mr. Latterlee." She hung up the phone. "Mr. Latterlee will see you in a few minutes."

I sat in that damn chair, sweating and squirming. I remembered what other kids told me about Mr. Latterlee. He would make you sit outside his office for a long time, to make you squirm in your chair thinking about the verbal lashing and awful punishment you were going to get. Kids told me how they had planned their verbal defenses, to play down their bad deeds. They had thought that they had outsmarted him, only to find out they hadn't.

Moment by moment, I waited nervously in my chair, until my dreaded time would come, when his secretary would say to me, "Mr. Latterley wants to see you in his office, now."

And here I was, sitting in that damn office chair, awaiting my sentence of doom, all because of a bunch of horses.

The secretary's telephone rang. "Certainly, I'll send him in."

With a smirk on her lips, "Mr. Latterlee will see *you* now," she said.

The guys were right, she really enjoys this.

When I got up out of my chair, my legs were weak. I could hardly walk, as I trembled from head to foot. Not knowing what would happen to me made my heart race madly as I hesitantly walked, step by step, towards his office. Each step I took felt like I was getting smaller as I walked to face my punishment. When I finally got to his door, he stared at me from behind his large wooden desk. He looked straight into my eyes, with an expression that indicated he was looking at a complete idiot. I feared what he was going to say. I looked down at the floor to escape his stare, thinking, *maybe he is right, I am an idiot.*

"Sit down," he commanded, as he rolled his chair up close to me and got right into my face. So close that I smelled his stinky hot breath—halitosis. Every time he talked, the smell penetrated up my nose, making me nauseous, like I was going to puke—puke right in his face. He stared at me through those thick glasses that made his eyes appear like big black olives.

He started his inquiry, shooting questions at me as fast as a machine gun.

Why did Mr. Lonzo send you down here?"

"I was late for school and I didn't have a note from home."

He opened his black spiral notebook and began writing some notes.

"You know the bell rings here at eight, where were you?"

"Up a tree surrounded by wild horses."

"That's preposterous! You better have a better alibi than that."

"I'm telling you the truth, Mr. Latterlee."

"Do you expect me to believe that tale?" He stood up and walked around to where I was seated and stared down at me through those thick frameless eyeglasses, dissecting me in his mind. "For the second time, where were you this morning?"

Those big dark olive eyes stared through his glasses, searching for the truth in my mind and on my face. *He's going to do what the kids had said, pull the truth out of my head. No matter what he tries, the answer will still be the same— stranded up in a tree, holding on for dear life.*

"Look at my torn pants, my cut hands from climbing the tree. Let me start at the beginning, Mr. Latterlee, I woke Mark up around six-thirty in the morning...."

(Sometime later)

Then he rolled his chair back behind his desk, and in deep thought, scratched his head with the few hairs left.

He's coming up with my punishment, one that I will always remember. I hope and pray that he doesn't say, "I'm going to call your parents in for a conference."

He stood up and walked away from his chair, faced me and said, "In all my years as a principal, I thought I had heard every possible excuse, but this one is so outlandish it has to be true." He walked back to his desk, sat down, and wrote something on a dark pink form. He handed it to me.

"Go back to class and give this to Mr. Lonzo."

I arrived back in my classroom, walked up to Mr. Lonzo and handed him my pass; it read: Excused—chased up a tree by a bunch of wild horses! Initialed, WGL

I knew one thing for sure, I wasn't going to get trapped in that pasture again and have to be sent to Mr. Latterlee's office all because of a bunch of wild horses.

Chapter 8

Murgatroyd

Mendham Borough, NJ 1948

The best part of growing up in the 40's and 50's was that we had to use our imagination and creativity during our time of play. That rang true for me growing up in a small country town of Mendham, in northern New Jersey. We didn't have a lot of toys and gadgets as children do today. Basically, boys had some sports items, such as; bats, balls and if you were lucky, a nice leather catcher's glove. Cowboy boots, pistols, and rifles were popular, as well. As for girls, I have absolutely no clue what they played with.

Historically at that time, the United States had ended the war, along with other nations, against Germany in 1945, the war known as World War II. As children, we heard our parents talk about the horrific battles, the devastating bombings, and the loss of lives. TV didn't come into most of our homes until the early 50's. News of the war was blasted every day out of our parents' radios and made daily headlines in the newspapers. We couldn't help overhear the awful war stories. The reality of war was imprinted in our young minds as children.

At school, we even had a bomb shelter, the school's basement. There were water and rations stored there too. We even had monthly air raid drills. The school buzzer would sound and each classroom would exit, in an orderly, and silent manner, to the school's bomb shelter. When we got to the basement, we had to sit on the floor and cover our heads with our hands.

It's no wonder that during outdoor play at home and at school in the playground, we battled the Germans. As kids, we had play guns; pistols, and rifles, but we most often would seek anything to make our battles more realistic. This was especially true for me growing up in the little village of Mendham, NJ.

One of my favorite memories was playing these imaginary battles with my friends, Al and Sam, who were twins.

My friends lived next to my home, our properties joined together, back to back, with a short dirt pathway that connected our two driveways. Al and Sam's parents always parked their beautiful black Packard, probably 1940 or thereabouts, on this interconnecting path. The Packard was built like a tank, believe me, a true American produced vehicle. The car had running boards on each side, huge front fenders, large external headlights, and a humungous chrome grill, with an interior featuring grey velour seats. Vehicles of this vintage had a manual shift, often called a stick shift. If my memory serves me right, the stick-shift was mounted on the floor. It was an H pattern shift, three-speeds forward and a reverse. To shift gears, the driver would have to press down the clutch pedal, shift, and release the pedal. The three pedals located left to right were; clutch, brake, and gas.

We had the greatest time planning out our imaginary attack against the Germans. When our plan was complete, we would all get into the Packard for our trip into a German sector. We had many serious battles with a few German troops, and sometimes, the three of us would take on an entire German troop brigade. It even got more exciting when we took on a few tanks! One of us would pretend to drive the Packard into battle. The driver would press down on the clutch and shift through the gears. When we met up with the enemy, the other two would roll the windows down and fire our weapons.

Sometimes, when the enemy was right at our heals, we would fight the battle using the car as a protective shield from the multitude of flying bullets. For our getaway, one of us would jump in the driver's seat, while the other two would stand on the running boards, holding onto the door handles, and shoot at our enemy. Another scene we played out, that one of us got captured by the Germans, tied up, and left in their garage. Later, two of us would crawl on our bellies approaching the garage, kill the guards, and release the captured prisoner, one of us. Of course, there was a major battle getting back to Murgatroyd, the 1940 Packard. Because of the newspaper headlines and the things we heard, it was important to us that the Germans be defeated.

64

We played this imaginary war battle often. One day, our little army of three decided that this Packard was such an outstanding war vehicle, that it had to have a special name. One of us, with the unanimous approval of the other two, came up with the name Murgatroyd. From that day on, this big black Packard, our war fortress, was called Murgatroyd.

I can't remember my buddies' parents ever driving Murgatroyd. I don't know what happened to it, but when I see one of those old Packard's, it conjures up great memories. None of us served in the military but seeing TV footage from the Korean and Vietnam wars brought back childhood memories of battle.

Chapter 9

The Farmall Tractor

Mendham Borough, NJ 1953-1955

Blizzards and Ice storms in the fifties were severe for those living in the small town of Mendham. It was common for residents to lose power for as much as two weeks at a time throughout the winter months. Power companies never asked for mutual aid from other power companies like they do today. Few families could afford an expensive portable generator. Those that didn't have one, used a fireplace or a pot stove to stay warm, fueling it with wood or big chunks of Anthracite Coal. They lit their homes with candles or oil lamps.

Some storms dumped three feet of snow or more with snow drifts up to six feet deep. Amounts like this required the Mendham's Road Department to continuously plow to keep up with the storm. There were times when the town's only plow truck broke down—roads stayed unplowed until the truck got fixed, sometimes days later. For residents, the arduous task of shoveling the driveway was dreaded. Working men got up early to shovel their driveways and put chains on their cars to travel to work. For smaller storms, some families used a multipurpose walk-behind tractor to plow snow. People that lived on Mendham Mountain found themselves stranded during some of the bigger storms because the plow truck could not make it up the mountain. The town had to clear the roads with a bulldozer. The operator had to be cautious when operating the dozer. If the bulldozer was tilted toward one side, it could slide like a sled off the mountain road. That happed a couple of times and left the bulldozer stranded until the snow melted and the ground hardened.

To deal with winter, my dad bought a powerful generator to power both houses and a large Farmall tractor to plow snow. We had nearly 1000 feet of driveway to clear. My older brother, Walter, saw dollar signs when Dad bought the tractor. He bought heavy duty steel chains for the tractor to plow local businesses. With chains, the Farmall was unstoppable. It was built like a tank and never broke down.

When my brother drove our tractor to plow for money, sometimes I accompanied him. I stood on the back drawbar, holding onto the operator's seat for dear life. The wind whipped across my face and my wet cotton-gloved hands would freeze stiff. When we got to a job site, my brother plowed; I shoveled to clear steps and sidewalks. After the jobs were completed, we drove home, my brother opened his wallet and handed me a few bucks—he got the better end of the deal.

As a young boy, my focus was on the tractor. I went to the haunted red barn to admire the fire engine red tractor several times a week—it was an addiction. I climbed up onto the seat, looked over the long hood, and pretended to drive it. The Farmall made a center stage in most of my dreams. They were happy dreams, not like the scary ones with ghosts chasing me.

During the summer, the only time the tractor got used was to even out the driveway gravel. That only happened once during the summer season. To keep the tractor battery charged, my dad had to start and run the tractor until the battery came up to a full charge. I sort of knew his schedule for doing that and followed him to the barn. He allowed me to stand on the back drawbar and watch him start it up. *I wondered what the ghosts thought when they heard that powerful Farmall running.* I watched him closely as he pushed in the clutch, slipped the transmission into neutral, pulled out the choke, and turned the key. The tractor always started immediately. His starting procedure burned into my brain the first time I watched him.

It was several months later, during the summer, that a persistent thought or desire to start the tractor came into in my head. The Jacobson fiasco was still fresh in my mind as I evaluated the risk of my idea and the dire consequences. I'm sure the episode of removing the gas motor from Dad's favorite lawnmower was still fresh in my Dad's mind, as well. He never forgot anything. Memories of my transgressions, adventures, and screw-ups must have taken up half of his brain. He remembered the details of all of them and could recite each in detail.

I thought, *should I add one more of my adventures to Dad's list? Was the thrill of starting the tractor worth the risk?*

My father was gone for the day on business and my mother was busy canning tomatoes. A perfect time to start the Farmall. It would be just the tractor and me; maybe also a ghost, if he wasn't sleeping. I nonchalantly walked to the barn and slid the barn door open. The door squeaked as it rolled along on the steel track. I stood there, in front of the tractor's dark green snow plow, admiring the massive grill, big engine, and huge tires. *Should I start it? It's not too late to back down. What happens if it starts up, goes backward right through the barn? Dad would have a shit-fit seeing a ten-foot hole in the side of the barn.* My heart raced in anticipation. *I'm going to do it! It will be my secret, along with the spirits that lurk in this barn.*

I walked to the second kitchen down in the cool basement where Mom was sterilizing Ball glass jars in a huge pot of boiling water. *I better tell her where I am going.*

"Mom, I'm going out to the barn find some wood to build something."

"I'll ring the bell when lunch is ready," she responded.

Before heading out, I glanced out the back window to make certain that Mom couldn't see the area in the barn where the tractor was garaged. It was well hidden with tall bushes three hundred feet back from the house. I stuck my head in the barn and checked for the ghost—all clear. Dad told me that gas engine exhaust fumes are deadly. *Maybe I should start the tractor with the door closed and get rid of that ghost.*

With my left hand on the large back tire and my other on the plow lever, I pulled myself up onto the tractor and sat down. On my right, was the long green lever that raised or lowered the plow. I looked over the long red hood as I held onto the steering wheel. Last month's memory came back to me, standing on the back and watching Dad start the tractor. Just sitting there made me feel ten years older, like an adult.

I must have sat in this seat hundreds of times in the past waiting until the day I would be old enough to drive the Farmall. Today, I would be halfway there. With that thought,

69

I pulled out the choke and watched the long rod that went along the side motor turn a lever on the carburetor. The throttle lever looked like it was set where it should be and the huge green plow was sitting on the cement floor. This would prevent the tractor from rolling when I put the shift lever in neutral and pushed down the clutch. I went to push in the clutch, but my leg was too short. I had to use the toe of my shoe to get it to go down. With my right hand, I grabbed the tall gear shift, searched through the 'H' pattern for neutral and placed the shift there. My heart pounded as I grabbed the key and turned it to start.

The starter engaged with the fan belt spinning around like mad. A puff of smoke rose from the exhaust as the engine started. *If my dad could see me now, he'd have a tizzy.* My foot was getting tired holding down the clutch, so I gently raised it, hoping that the tractor would not suddenly lurch forward or worse yet, go backward through the side of the barn. It was reassuring to see it stayed parked and just idled away.

Do I drive it a few feet forward? What if it stalls out and detective Dad notices that it's not parked in the same spot he parked it? This event would be out of the universe compared to borrowing the engine from his favorite lawnmower. I'm so much in trouble now, I might as well add one more thing and drive it a few feet.

To do that, I had to lift the heavy six-foot wide plow off the garage floor. With my right hand, I pulled the plow lever—it didn't budge. With two hands, I grabbed the lever and pulled back with all my strength. The plow lifted off the cement and locked into place.

Back on the seat, I confidently pushed in the clutch, shifted into first gear, and slowly let out the clutch. The huge tractor moved forward like a tank. Before I knew it, it had traveled completely out the garage. *Damn, damn, damn....didn't want to do that. Got to get this back into the barn before anyone sees it.* Going forward seemed simple, but going backward proved not to be as simple—I couldn't see the pedals. If my toe slipped off the clutch, the tractor would plow with ease through the side of the garage. *Dad would sure follow through with his threat of sending me off to military school.*

I reduced the throttle speed and reversed the tractor into the garage. In horror I thought, *how do I stop this thing? Turn the key off!* My hand turned the key and the tractor came to a complete stop. I grabbed the lever and dropped the plow. I had achieved my Farmall adventure for now, hopefully without my father finding out.

I took a two-year break from doing anything more on a solo basis with the tractor. The next milepost would be driving it, and I didn't have a plan on how I could pull that off.

One day, two years later, my mother and a friend were shopping in Morristown and Dad was at work I decided to get behind the wheel of the tractor for a trip around the yard. I had taken the shortcut through my buddies' property that landed me right in front of the red barn. Being two years older since I last turned the key, the tractor had seemed to get a little smaller.

Starting it was easy and before long, I was headed out of the barn going past my brother's house and approaching mine. Nobody was around as I enjoyed the scenery sitting up high in the seat. When I got past my house, I made a left to go up the hill and around the circular driveway in front of my house. I looked up ahead and there was my sister, Wilma, standing there on her side lawn. I couldn't tell if she was worried or surprised to see me driving—maybe both.

As I completed the circle, I decided to make another lap and made a right to go up the hill. My sister was gone. There was no way she could contact Mom or Dad, but she could call the police—my brother. I saw her peer out her kitchen window and watch me. There was lots of gas in the tank and at least an hour or two of safe time for my excursion. For a greater thrill, I pushed down the clutch and shifted to second gear. Wow! It seemed like I was zipping around the property, but in reality, it was still pretty slow.

Later that day, my parents were home, ready to sit down for dinner, but there was no mention of me driving the Farmall. My sister had kept my secret. My driving the tractor became a special event, repeated several times, until my dad sold it.

Many years later, after I married and had a family, Dad and I sat down to have a beer. We were talking about the tractor and he looked up at me with a slight smile and said, "You know that I knew you were driving that tractor, don't you?"

"You always were a great detective, Dad."

And we raised our beers to salute one another.

Chapter 10

We Dare You!

Mendham Borough, NJ 1954

Halloween had arrived and the three Mendham musketeers, Al, Sam, and I decided to have some fun. The three of us were around 12 years old and it must have been my idea, since I ate and slept experimental electronics. The idea was to charge small electrolytic capacitors with a high direct current voltage and then dare some poor kid to touch the two leads.

For those that have no background in electronics, a capacitor is an electronic component. Its physical shape is tubular in various diameters and it's made in various lengths. An electrical connection is made with either two or more electrical leads (wires) or metal tabs. This device is normally used in electronic power supplies, which smooths out pulsating direct currents to a steady direct current. It also stores an electrical voltage for a period of time until it slowly discharges. That fact was what gave me the idea for a Halloween prank.

This took place on the sidewalk in front of the big white house on Main Street in Mendham, NJ. This was the Larson's house, a landmark of Mendham and my parent's previously owned home. The sidewalk was boarded by a beautiful stone wall made of reddish oval stones that had been imported from another country and cemented in place.

Children always flocked to the Larson's home because they always gave the best treats. This year it was ice cream cones in several flavors. It didn't take long for the tasty news to spread and every kid headed for the Larson's house.

Before kids got to the front door, the three of us offered the trick or treaters some delicious candy if they touched the two little wires of a very small capacitor. To the kids, this was a win-win situation. We had brought several capacitors inside to charge them up to about a hundred volts and needed to use great care not to shock ourselves. The first victim eagerly grabbed the two leads and got knocked on his ass.

73

He didn't even ask for our candy bar, he just took off crying loudly. We couldn't contain our laughter. Soon, another unsuspecting kid took the capacitor challenge and he got knocked on his ass, too. This trick went on for some time until one of us volunteered to see what the shock felt like. We argued back and forth on who would play the victim.

"Well, since it was your great idea, Greg, you should play the Halloween kid," said Al.

"Are you kidding—not me!"

"How about I go inside, get a hat and write our name on three bits of paper," Sam suggested.

"Sounds good to me," Al said, patting me on the back. "Okay with you Greg?"

"I guess so."

Sam went inside and came out a short time later with a navy blue Yankee's cap. "Here we are, guys. Greg, you get first to pick. Let me mix the papers around, I don't want you to think I rigged your selection." After several twirls of his fingers, he shoved the hat at me. "Pick."

Hoping that luck was with me, I picked out a paper as Al turned on his flashlight to see the name—'GREG.' Chuckling, Al held out the capacitor for me to grab as Sam watched in anticipation of me being shocked. I grabbed the leads.

"Ow! Holy crap, that nearly killed me!" I said laying on the ground, as Al and Sam were laughing their heads off.

After I got up, the idea came to me to check the other two pieces of paper left in the hat. "Al, bring that flashlight over here so I can see the other two papers." I pulled out one and opened it up—GREG. "What!" Then I pulled out the last piece—GREG. "You dirty dog, Sam," as I chased him around the yard until we were both exhausted.

Chapter 11

The Little Cannon

Mendham Borough, NJ 1956

One of my best childhood memories happened on Mischief Night in the little country town of Mendham. My best friends, Al and Sam Larson, who were neighbors, came over to visit me one afternoon, the day before Halloween. Their dad had gone on a business trip to South America the previous week and brought back a gift for his twin sons, a cannon about 18-inches long. This cannon was neat; it was ruggedly made with a steel barrel and two cast steel spoke wheels. The best part, it worked! To fire it, you inserted a string fuse, filled the barrel with black gunpowder (the more the better—our motto), secured the gunpowder with a wad of cotton, and lit the fuse. Moments later, the gunpowder would ignite. The blast was deafening—heard at least a half-mile away.

When the three of us got together, we always came up with all sorts of interesting things to do. It was the day before Halloween and we decided to do something unusual for Mischief Night.

"Got any ideas for the big night?" Al asked me.

"Not a clue. Remember, my brother, Walter, is the police chief in town."

"What's he going to do, throw his kid brother in the slammer? I don't think so," Al replied.

"If I were him, I'd do just that," Sam chimed in with a chuckle.

"We could sneak around in the dark and do something for laughs, you know, maybe spray shaving cream on a few cars," Al suggested.

"Every kid in town does that. We need to do something new, something that will be remembered for years to come; maybe even make the newspapers." I said.

It didn't take long for us to come up with a brilliant idea. The decision was to use the twins newly acquired cannon to scare the wits out of our unsuspecting neighbors.

After dinner, on Mischief Night, we all got together to prepare for the evening's fun activity. We gathered up a jar of gunpowder, a ball of string, a large wad of cotton, and a Boy Scout knife. We sat on the twins' front porch talking, laughing, and checking the clock for 'mission-hour.' Al went into his house to check the clock for the millionth time, then ran out the door and said, "It is time to roll!"

We moved the cannon to our first neighbor's home, right in front of their front door. One of us served as a lookout; another the doorbell ringer, and the third guy, the fuse igniter. It was planned that we would run and hide after igniting the fuse when no one was roaming around outside. Since the cannon was the twins, I rang the doorbell and Sam lit the fuse. We ran and hid behind some bushes and placed our hands over our ears. BOOM!

We peeked out from the bushes and saw a guy who stood there in a state of shock. He probably thought he had been shot. Moments later, when he realized that he had survived the explosion, he quickly slammed the front door shut—probably to call the police.

We cautiously moved-up to the house to retrieve our cannon. A black cloud of smoke still hung around it. Sam ran up, grabbed the cannon and joined the two of us as we escaped into the safety of darkness. As we ran, laughing hysterically, we realized we had to do it again. This was a blast to do— literally! Not wanting to get caught in the act, we went a few blocks away to ring the next doorbell. As the evening went on, we were running low on gunpowder after frightening seven neighbors. We only had enough gunpowder for maybe two more pranks. For our last victim, we decided we had to do it at my house, to my dad.

My dad was strict as hell and would get bent out of shape very easily. When he got upset over something, he'd get very boisterous, and yell out a stream of threats. We all agreed, an excellent victim. We broke out in laughter anticipating his reaction. Only one problem, we just couldn't get caught.

♐

About a year prior to this mischief night, my much older brother, Walter, held the position as Chief of Police in Mendham. Chief Smith had been successful in getting funding for a two-way radio system, along with a contract for Mendham to use the services of Morris County's Police Radio System. This allowed Mendham residents to have 24-hour telephone contact with the police. At the time, there was no 24-hour, 7-day a week dispatcher at headquarters. Mendham was one of the first towns in the county to sign-up for this service. Several months prior to mischief night, Mendham installed the new radio equipment in its only Ford Interceptor patrol car and a base radio at the police station.

Mischief night was the most active night for mysterious things to happen in town. Almost yearly, an outhouse would somehow appear the next morning at the Route 24 traffic light in the middle of the town. Some years, a small foreign car would find its way on the Post Office's front steps or some other ridiculous place. The huge grammar school flagpole usually had something humorous hanging proudly at the top it. One year, someone raised a full size stuffed manikin that was dressed in farmer's attire.

There was usually so much mischief that the police department would enlist their special officers. These were part-time officers who had minimal police training. On this night, they would use their own vehicles. Each vehicle would have amateur radio equipment temporarily installed, along with a ham radio operator. Some were Bell Labs engineers and a few were high school students with FCC (Federal Communications Commission) ham (radio amateur) licenses. Mendham Borough's police car would also have a ham radio system and operator. With the additional cars, patrolling the town worked well to a point. Still, silly things happened in good fun.

♐

Mischief night my brother was on patrol with his group of specials along with the ham radio operators. They kept an eye on the town, patrolling to keep law and order. Suddenly, his radio came alive.

"Morris County dispatch to Mendham Borough."

"Mendham Borough, go ahead," replied Chief Smith.

"Morris County Radio, we have several reports of three kids going around your town ringing doorbells and firing off a cannon at residents. Also, there're residents reporting loud explosions or gunfire, over."

"Morris County, this is Mendham, I have a good idea who these three characters are, over."

"10-4, Morris County, out."

In the meantime, the three of us arrived at my parent's house for the grand finale. My house had a semi-enclosed front porch about twenty feet wide that covered the front door entrance. The porch light was out because it was late in the evening and the trick or treat youngsters had all gone home. We set the cannon on the top stair landing and lit a longer fuse. I rang the doorbell in a persistent and annoying manner; then the three of us ran to hide behind a tall hedge. We pushed the branches open to watch my father's reaction. A couple of minutes later, my dad flicked on the front porch light and appeared at the opened door—timing is everything. Just as he appeared at the door, the cannon roared with the most ungodly awful explosion. BOOM! We must have put an extra amount of gunpowder in the barrel for good measure. The sound never seemed to end as it reverberated and echoed back and forth on the porch. As we ran away and glanced back at my father, we saw he was covered in black gun powder residue that looked like soot. He bellowed out, "I know who you are! I'm calling the police! You're going to be in a hell of a lot of trouble!"

My dad slammed the door shut and I took-off to retrieve the cannon. With the cannon in my arms, the three of us cautiously moved in the cover of the bushes and trees a distance away, so as to remain concealed. Later on, I headed home. When I arrived, my mother and father were waiting for me—neither looked very happy. Dad looked at me, still riled-up in a fit of anger.

"You know, your father has a bad heart. This could have killed him," Mom said.

"Sorry, Dad."

"Sorry? You're in a hell of a lot of trouble, not only with me, but the police. They're out looking for all three of you now," yelled, Dad.

"Sure, Dad. And how do you know that?"

"From your brother. He's going to pull all of you into police headquarters tomorrow to interrogate you. Morris County radio put out an APB on the three of you. Get to your room! You're grounded!"

My brother and his wife resided in a second home on my parent's property. Overnight, Mendham's police car would be parked there. I snuck out of the house the next morning, seeing the police car in the driveway, I hung around outside their house and waited for my brother to go to work. When the back door opened and my brother came down the steps dressed in his police uniform, I ran up to him as he approached the police car and said:

"So, a Walter, a....when do you want the three of us to come to police headquarters?"

He walked up close to me, looked me straight in the eyes, and appeared to be thinking of what to say to me.

"I'm going to give you a break this time and not bring you into the station, but I never want to see or hear that cannon again. That goes for the Larson twins, too, and be sure to tell them that."

"I promise never to use that cannon again—scouts honor. I'm really lucky to have you as my cool brother.

"Okay, let this be a good lesson," he said, as he got into the police car and drove away.

I stood there and watched him leave, all the while thinking about what the three of us could do next year to top this.

Chapter 12

The X-ray Machine

Mendham Borough, NJ 1952

Another memorable moment happened when I was in fifth grade. My best friends, Al and Sam Larson, who were my neighbors, came over to visit one afternoon. We met down in the spare kitchen located in the basement. This kitchen my mom used to can or freeze our garden vegetables to use in the winter months. This room stayed much cooler than our main kitchen during stifling hot summer days. The kitchen had a double sink with running water and a stove.

This turned out to be a great room for the three junior scientists to use as an experimental laboratory. We explored all sorts of wild ideas in the field of chemistry and electronics. Our material resource for doing chemistry experiments was a Gilbert Chemistry set. This set included a wealth of various chemicals contained in small glass jars, test tubes, and other chemistry apparatus. All these items were neatly stored in a metal case. Our inventory of electronic parts came from discarded radios that we found along the road, put out for the garbage man. Additional radios were bought at church auctions for less than a dollar. The ones that didn't sell were free for the taking after the auction ended. Electronic parts, transformers, resistors, and capacitors were unsoldered and thrown into cardboard boxes for later use.

We had a great time building electronic projects. Besides simple crystal radios, we built circuits that used high voltage components, such as vacuum tubes. This turned out to be a shocking experience on more than one occasion–literally! One day, we all decided to each build a high voltage power supply on a wood board. Each of us grabbed a power transformer from our parts inventory, along with other components. The transformers were heavy, they were constructed with numerous steel plates and internally had multiple copper wire windings and were about a four-inch cube in size.

We spent the day mounting parts onto a wooden board, then soldered them together to make a high voltage DC power supply circuit. The last part of the project was to solder on the 120-volt line cord. That afternoon, we had all finished our projects and proudly placed our finished power supplies on the kitchen table. They sat all in a row like treasured trophies. After all our hard work, it was time to plug each one in to see if it worked. I remember my father's departing words before he left for work. Dad shouted down the basement steps to me:

"Don't set the house on fire! Do you hear me?"

Sam was the first one up, he plugged his unit into the electrical outlet. The power supply did absolutely nothing. Al went next. His hummed and that was a good sign that it worked. Then it was my turn. I pushed the plug into the outlet. Sparks immediately flew out of the outlet, burning my hand. The transformer smoked, and small flames shot out from numerous places around the transformer from the copper coil area. I quickly unplugged the power supply and carried the smoldering and burning power supply outside. *Don't burn the house down,* rattled through my head. But, it was too late to air out the awful smell that had saturated the kitchen and rose quickly up the stairway to the main floor

A few minutes later, my mom was at the top of the stairs, "What in the world are you doing down there? It stinks to high heavens! There's no power in half the house!"

"I'll take care of it." So off to the fuse box I went with a flashlight. It was on the other side of the house, down under a crawl space, mounted on a cement block wall. There were only six fuses for the entire house in the fuse box. Dad had lined a row of new fuses across the top of the steel fuse box. I had killed most of the new ones and put the blown ones back where the good ones should have been placed. I knew sometime, in the near future, that my dad would have to replace a fuse and find that every damn spare fuse was blown, which would produce a shit-fit for sure.

We also built some pretty impressive scientific devices, such as a Van de Graaff, a super high voltage, spark generator. This hand-cranked generator developed such a high voltage that it produced a stream of two-inch sparks that jumped between two electrodes. It truly made the three of us feel like mad scientists.

I suggested that it would be cool to see our bones beneath our skin, perhaps the ones in our hand. Everyone unanimously agreed that this would be a fun thing to do. To do this, we would need to build an X-ray machine. As we conversed with one another, we discussed the most difficult part would be to construct an X-ray tube that emitted the invisible rays. We had no idea on how to construct the tube. Since I came up with the idea, I volunteered to do the scientific investigation on how an X-ray tube worked and how it was constructed. Back then, to research something, you had to look it up in your home encyclopedia or go to our small-town library.

I chose to go to the library since they had the newest encyclopedia. At the library they didn't allow you to take home the encyclopedia, you usually took notes which took forever. For diagrams, you had to bring carbon paper with you. It was very messy. To make copies of circuits or diagrams you had to be vigilant, making sure the librarian wasn't in the area. If the coast was clear, you traced the diagram in the book onto a sheet of paper using carbon paper. If you got caught marking the book, you got fined.

That night, after dinner, I got to work reading and taking more notes from my parent's older Encyclopedia Britannica. The technical level of the information was far beyond my understanding. But, I was able to glean enough of the information to construct a simple X-ray tube. The tube needed to be glass, filled with mercury vapor, fitted with two metal plate electrodes, and the assembly needed to be evacuated of air. The tube had to be powered by a very high voltage power supply so that X-rays would emit off the tube's plates.

Construction began the next morning. Sam, Al, and I selected a used radio tube to obtain two metal plate electrodes. For the glass tube, we grabbed a test tube and a rubber stopper from the Gilbert Chemistry set. Next, we needed mercury—where were we going to obtain mercury? Then the thought came to me, our family's medical thermometer, the one my mother used to check if I had a fever.

I went upstairs to the main bathroom and snatched the thermometer. The last item we needed was the metal shield. We located a discarded steel can in my parent's garbage can that would work well. We could easily cut the can with tin snips to make an effective radiation shield.

Construction began immediately. First, we wrapped the old tube in cloth and smashed the glass to extricate the internal metal plates. Next, we poked two holes in the rubber stopper and pushed the plate wires through the holes. Sam snapped off the tip of the thermometer and captured the bead of mercury into a jar lid. The last step was to seal the tube, evacuate the air, and vaporize the mercury.

Time for a technical meeting. How were we ever going to evacuate the tube? Al was the first one to come up with a simple method. Drop a bead of mercury into the test tube, place the stopper a little loose, heat the test tube with the alcohol burner, and secure the stopper when the mercury vaporized.

Sidebar: Mercury is extremely toxic to the human body and can lead to death.

It took all of our six skillful hands to hold, heat, evacuate, and seal the X-ray tube. Minutes later we finished. Success! We all proudly admired the cooled down X-ray tube with the mercury flashed vapor.

To operate the X-ray tube, we needed a high voltage power supply. Our first thought was to use the Van de Graaff generator, but that generated too much voltage. I suggested that we build one. But, where would we find a high voltage transformer? An idea came to me.

"Guys, remember the transformer experiment we did a few months ago?"

"Which one was that?" said Sam.

"I'm surprised you forgot, Sam. That's the one you accidentally brushed up against two wires and got knocked on your ass."

"You're right, how could I ever forget that experience?"

"We learned if we plugged in a step-down transformer backward into a house outlet, it became a step-up transformer generating several hundred volts on the output wires."

The next week, we located some parts and fabricated the high voltage power supply. At the end of the week, everything was coming together. We had built the stand for the X-ray tube and connected it to the power supply. The last detail was to make the photography plates.

For that, we cut several 3" by 3" sections of black construction paper. We needed an undeveloped film. With my 35-cent weekly allowance, there was no way I could come up with the money to buy a new roll of film. The only source of unexposed film was in my Kodak Brownie camera. We took it into the dark photography room, opened the camera, unrolled the film, cut the film to size, and sealed the unexposed film between the two pieces of black construction paper. We had just finished, when my mother yelled down the cellar stairs, "Dinner is ready."

"Guys, let's meet after dinner and fire-up the X-ray machine," I suggested.

"After all of our work, it will be great to see if it penetrates our skin, right down to the bones," Al said.

"Don't ask me to put my hand underneath that thing," Sam added.

"Maybe we should draw names out of a hat, old buddy," I kiddingly said.

"Not a chance," retorted Sam.

Sam and Al arrived at their home. As they opened the door they could smell it, boiled lobsters and corn on the cob. Their mother had a lobster and an ear of corn on each plate. Sam and Al joined their older sister and brother at the table. Everyone got bibbed and ready to eat. Doctor Larson and his wife were seated and began breaking the claws off their lobsters. He took his tiny fork and dug out the claw meat, just before he was going to put it in his mouth he asked, "What constructive things did you fellows do today?"

Sam blurted out, "The three junior scientists built an X-ray machine! We're going to check-out our bones!"

"Sam! You idiot! That was supposed to be a secret!" Al shouted!"

"That's idiotic! X-rays! X-rays are lethal! Where is that machine?" Yelled Dr. Larson.

"Down in Greg's basement," said Sam, sheepishly.

"There's no way the three of you are going to fool around with that!"

Dr. Larson got up from the table, threw-down his bib and headed for the back door.

After dinner, I went downstairs to our laboratory in the basement kitchen and waited for the twins. When I reached the bottom step, I looked over at the table where we had set-up our X-ray machine—it was gone! Someone stole it!

I buzzed them on our private telephone system between our houses. "Al! Someone stole our X-ray machine!"

"That's not what happened. We were having our dinner and Dad asked us what we did today. Sam blurted out, we built an X-ray machine and we're going to use it to check out the bones in our hand. Dad got up from the dinner table and headed straight for your house. He came back here and smashed the X-ray tube and threw everything into our garbage can."

"After all that work! I guess we're just going to start on a new project," I said.

"Got any bright ideas that won't end up in the garbage can?" Al asked.

"How about something useful, like an electrical hotdog cooker? We could use two insulated wood strips of nails, jab the hotdogs on each end, and plug them into an outlet. Shooting 120 volts into those suckers they'd get done no time!" I suggested.

So that ended our X-ray machine project and medical bone curiosity for the three of us junior scientists, but the next project would be on the bench soon—most likely the next day!

Chapter 13

The Second Amendment

Mendham Borough, NJ 1952

Most of us kids growing up in Mendham had a B-B gun. Cowboy shows like *Gene Autry* and *The Lone Ranger* entertained us daily on the radio and years later on TV. We often reenacted scenes from these shows or wrote our own stories—where the good guy always prevailed. As kids, we explored the woods carrying our B-B rifles over our shoulders. During our outings, we often came across wildlife, especially rabbits, innocently munching on some grass. We snuck up, aimed, and fired our guns at them. With our poor aim and the gun's poor accuracy, none were ever hit. They just ran away and hid in the bushes. During the summer months, box turtles appeared once in awhile in our yards. Garter snakes were occasionally around, too and if you raised farm animals, large black snakes were found slithering around the property.

Another buddy of mine, Jerry, had a real gun, a 22-caliber rifle that shot 22 longs and shorts. The longs were for more distant targets and the shorts for closer range. Jerry had an outdoor shooting range consisting of several bales of hay stacked up in his backyard. A target with colored rings was secured in place on the center bale. Al, Sam and I often watched Jerry doing target practice in his backyard. His mother always sat in the family car supervising his target practice.

One day, Jerry asked us if we would like to shoot his gun. All of us got really excited for that opportunity. Jerry handed the rifle to Al, as Sam and I intently watched. He gave us the usual safety talk. Part of Jerry's persona was to chuckle after making an important statement.

"Don't be an idiot and point the gun at anyone," chuckle. "The second rule, always point the gun down at the ground, not at your feet either," chuckle. "To load it, you pull back the bolt, slide the shell into the barrel and engage the bolt.

Don't cock-it until you're ready to fire," chuckle. "Everyone must stay behind the shooter," chuckle.

"Jerry's mother, seeing the possible danger, got out of her car and stood to supervise the four of us. We all got behind Al as he inserted the shell, cocked the gun, aimed, and pulled the trigger—POW! Looking at the target, we thought it was an accurate hit. Jerry's mother took possession of the gun while we ran down to check the target. Al, with a proud grin and expanded chest, pointed to the red center ring where his shot landed.

"Great shot!" his brother, Sam exclaimed.

"Ah, beginners' luck," I commented.

We all scooted back for Sam to take his turn. Jerry's mom handed Sam the rifle, he loaded it like a pro. He aimed and took his shot. He handed the gun over to Jerry's mom while we ran to check out the target. It landed just outside the red circle. My heart started banging away as I thought, *my turn's next.*

Back at the firing position, Jerry's mom handed me the rifle. I was bursting with excitement holding a real gun. Jerry handed me a shell, my hand shook with so much anticipation that I dropped it. I knelt down to pick it up and accidentally swung the gun barrel up, right towards Jerry.

Jerry's mom grabbed the barrel forcing it to point back down and yelled, "What did Jerry tell you? Always point the gun down at the ground!"

Embarrassed at my mistake, I got up, removed Sam's spent shell and reloaded. I checked to make sure everyone was in the back of me. My left eye peered through the sight at the target, trying to aim for the small red ring. I shook so much, the red dot kept moving. My friends anxiously waited for their turns again, yelling for me to shoot.

"Would you pull the trigger?" Jerry shouted.

"What are you waiting for?" Sam asked.

Under pressure from my friends, I aimed for the target, held my breath, and squeezed the trigger—POW! I handed the rifle to Jerry's mom and took off running towards the target.

90

Bursting with excitement, *I've just shot a real gun! How cool is that? Can't wait for my next turn!*

I arrived first at the target, there were only two holes at the center, none mine. But outside all the rings on the white border was a single hole, mine. I lowered my head in disappointment.

"At least you hit the paper!" Jerry chuckled.

"Looks like the bandit got away," Sam joined in laughing.

Al patted me on the back and said, "You'll get better next time."

The next hour we continued to take turns until the small shell container was empty. On my way home, I planned to tell my parents about shooting a real gun. On further thought, I had second thoughts, *Dad would have a tizzy and I would be banned from going to Jerry's house again. Plus, I would get a good talking to.*

After shooting the 22, I had no urge to ever use my puny B-B gun ever again. I couldn't wait to tell my brother, Walter, about my experience. He happened to be Mendham Borough's Police Chief, as well as, an avid hunter and would keep my secret from our parents.

Wanting a real gun, I remembered seeing a rifle some time ago in my brother's old room. *Would the rifle still be there?* I opened his closet door and shuffled stuff inside. My hand landed on a cold steel barrel. I pulled it out and inspected it. It was a single shot, bolt action 22 caliber rifle. There was some rust on the steel areas including the barrel and the gun looked old. *Was it loaded?* I pulled back the bolt and checked to see if it was loaded. *Nope; I'll ask Dad later when he gets home if I could have it—fat chance!*

It was about six when I heard Dad's car going over our gravel driveway towards the haunted red barn, where Dad garaged his car. I waited until Dad came through the back door.

"Hi, Dad, did you have a good day? *If it was, I was about to ruin it,* I thought.

91

"It was great! I sold a large order of industrial coatings to a company in Pennsylvania."

"Terrific. Dad, there's an old rusty gun in Walter's former bedroom, may I have it?"

"Absolutely not! Are you crazy? Guns are dangerous—not for kids!"

"But, Dad! The Second Amendment of the Constitution says I have the right to own a gun and bear arms. I learned that at school this week, Dad."

"The Second Amendment doesn't apply to children, for God's sake."

"This gun's broken, rusty, and will never work in a million years. P-l-e-a-s-e, just look at it." I ran to get it from the closet, grabbed it, and showed it to my father. "See, Dad?"

"This was your brother's old gun. I'll remove the firing pin so it can't be fired. You must treat this gun as if it were real. If I see you messing around with it in an unsafe manner, it will be taken away for good, is that understood?"

"Yes, Dad."

Later Dad took the gun and hid it somewhere in the house. The next morning when I arrived in the kitchen for breakfast, Dad had it ready for me. It was propped up in the corner against the wall. He picked it up and held it pointing at the floor.

"Before I give you the gun, I'm going to teach you gun safety. Never point the gun at anyone. Always make sure the gun is unloaded. Always have the bolt open. Never take the gun off our property."

Dad handed me the gun and left for work. I was so happy to have my very own rifle and couldn't wait to tell all my friends at school!

As I walked into my fifth-grade homeroom, Mrs. Martin, my teacher, was sitting behind her desk pushing some papers around. She looked at me and said, "Greg, you look so happy today. Something wonderful must have happened this morning." She really emphasized the word wonderful.

I nearly said, "Yeah, I just got a real gun!" *That would have been suicide, she'd have sent me down to Mr. Latterlee's office in a flash.* Mr. Latterlee was our principal, the scariest man you ever saw. Kids avoided him like the plague. If they saw him in the hallway, they would head the other way.

No, I'm not going to tell Mrs. Martin I have a real gun. I'm not going through that ordeal!

After school, I waited for my friends Al and Sam to arrive at the sidewalk in front of the school. They came out the front door and headed towards me. I ran up to them and whispered, "Guys, my dad gave me a real 22 rifle."

"Your father would never, ever give you a rifle," Al exclaimed.

"You're just pulling our leg," Sam added.

"He gave me the gun this morning. He took the firing pin out so it couldn't be fired. I looked in the school's library encyclopedia after lunch, to see how a firing pin worked. I think we can make one," I replied.

"What does a firing pin look like?" asked Sam.

"It's just a slim piece of metal that has a spring on one end and sort of a sharp point on the other end. We can make one out of a flat flooring nail by filing it down. To test it out, we can get a 22 from Jerry."

Later in the barn, I was at the vise filing the nail to fit the rifle. I had tried it several times, but it was still too big. After I filed it again and slid it into the slot it got stuck. With a small screwdriver and hammer, I drove it out. *Just a little bit more.* The twins watched as I carefully filed a small amount of metal off the pin. Sam held the bolt, while I slid the firing pin into place.

We cocked the rifle without a shell, pulled the trigger, and heard the firing pin slide home with a loud click. We took the gun outside, Al removed the shell from his pocket that he got from Jerry and placed it into the barrel.

He handed the gun back to me. My buddies got behind me and stood to watch as I cocked it, aimed for the ground and pulled the trigger—nothing happened.

After we tried to fire the gun without success, we gave up, something was wrong. We walked back to the red barn, kept a wide birth from the spooky wood doors on the floor, and headed for the tool room. We pulled three stools together and sat trying to figure out what was wrong.

"Well, that was a big flop," Al remarked.

"It should have worked," I responded.

Sam held the gun, cocked it, and pointed it at the cement floor. He pulled the trigger—nothing happened.

Al grabbed it from Sam, got up, walked to the doorway, cocked the gun, and aimed it at one of the wood floor panels. "Come out you haunted, evil beast!" He pulled the trigger, the gun failed to fire. He cocked the gun again, ready for the haunted soul to peak out from under the panel—nothing. Without thinking, he left the gun cocked, ready to fire.

After his attempt to scare whatever might be down there, he rejoined us in the tool room. He leaned the gun against the workbench. As we chatted away, we passed the gun around not being very careful where it was pointed, even at times at one another. Sometimes we even had our fingers on the trigger making believe we were firing the gun—shouting, POW! Just holding a real gun felt great.

The gun was in my hands, when I pointed it at the ceiling, and pulled the trigger and the gun fired—POW!

"My God! That could have killed one of us!" I yelled.

"I forgot I left it loaded," Al sheepishly said.

"That was really stupid! Why the hell did you leave the gun loaded?" yelled Sam.

"Greg should have checked to make sure it wasn't loaded before he pulled the trigger! Do you realize one of us could have been killed?" Al retorted in a mad tone.

"Well no one got killed, but one of us is going to get killed when my dad sees the hole in the ceiling," I said.

"Tell him we were shooting at the ghost," Sam suggested.

Dad never noticed the small hole in the ceiling, luckily it didn't put a hole in the steel corrugated roof, since the bullet lodged itself in the second story roof rafter.

Chapter 14

Call the Press!

Mendham Borough, NJ 1955

This story began before I was born, sometime after the 1929 Great Depression. If you ever take a road trip out on Route 1-24W, to or through Mendham, you can try to spot this two-story, center hall colonial home, often called the 'Big House,' where this true story took place. Details, with the passing of time, remain foggy at best, but old-timers, still enjoy sharing this story with younger folks. Most younger folks can't begin to imagine the hardship this country went through during the Great Depression. The post-depression mindset set this story in motion.

The horrific collapse of the US economy, the bank failures, home foreclosures, and worthless stocks caused great hardships for American families for years. The stock market collapse on Wall Street resulted in some heavy investors doing drastic things. Consumed and devastated by their complete financial loss, some committed suicide; jumped out of tall buildings or took the easy way out—a gunshot to the head.

Following the Great Depression, people no longer trusted banks. They kept their cash close by with their personal possessions. Some actually kept it under their mattresses. Others were more creative, hiding it inside a wall, in the attic, or even burying it in the backyard.

Many families, including those in Mendham, had gone through the Great Depression, lost all their savings, their jobs, and even their homes. They were homeless and destitute. As they rebuilt their lives from scratch, they learned a good lesson—don't trust banks. In most marriages of the time, husbands were in charge of family finances. They were coined family providers, heads of household, gatekeepers of the money.

For this elderly couple living in the 'big house,' the husband oversaw all their finances.

97

He trusted no one including his wife. He hid the accumulated fortune and he hid it well, where no one would find it. Well, he died unexpectedly one night. The next morning his wife found him, with his lips sealed forever.

After the undertaker removed his body that morning, she went on a frantic search, from the attic to the basement without finding his elusive hiding spot. She continued searching for secret compartments in furniture and even checking for loose bricks in the massive fireplace. With no money to pay her living expenses, including her husband's funeral, she moved out of the house. The 'For Sale' sign went up shortly after, but it had taken a long time to sell the house.

It didn't take long though, for the rumor to spread, that a cache of money had been hidden somewhere on the property and remained unfound. People, desperate for cash, broke into the house to search for the loot. Neighbors reported seeing burglars looking for the money. One neighbor even reported seeing a ghost up on the second floor. It was rumored that this was the old miser coming back from the grave to make sure that his money was still safe.

The break-ins became a big problem for realtors. When they came to show the property to a prospective buyer, they never knew the condition of the home. There were times when walls were torn open, toilets dismantled and the elegant oak staircases ripped apart, and other extreme acts of damage. Some thought the wealthy guy was smart, knew the robbers would look first in the house, albeit not in the yard.

The house changed ownership a couple of times before my family bought it in the early 1940's. My parents not only bought the house, but also the lure of the lost fortune. They, along with my much older sister and brother, sometimes had a hunch where the money might be hidden, but after investigating, always came away empty handed.

I was about two when my parents could no longer afford the home and sold it to buy the farm property behind the Big House. It consisted of a large parcel of land, about 40 acres, two smaller homes, and a few barns. What made the real estate interesting, were the barns. Two were haunted and later torn down, but whoever haunted them had moved to the huge two-story red barn.

My brother, Walter, having recently married, lived in one of the houses, behind the 'big house' and close to the ghost-inhabited barn. He had a green thumb and enjoyed vegetable gardening and growing beautiful flowers. We lived in the other house, about a hundred feet away. Being neighbors, I would often see him working in the yard. On this day, my brother was in the process of planting a large flowering bush near his house. The bush had a protective burlap cover over the extensive root ball. It sat on the lawn near the area he intended to plant it. He had brought out a shovel from the garage and walked around the lawn to find the best spot to plant it.

"Right here, this is the spot," he said to me.

As a nine-year-old kid, I stood there watching him digging the hole. We were shooting the breeze, talking about vacation time, going to Barnegat Light. The hole was getting to be the right size in diameter for the large root ball, but needed to be deeper. The ground was hard, so my brother retrieved a pick from the garage to break-up the dirt. He raised the pick and swung it down into the hole. It bounced back making an odd sound, "clunk."

"Hit something, probably some buried piece of junk," he said.

"It sure didn't sound like a rock," I commented.

He continued to remove more dirt. With each shovel, the piece of junk appeared to be a thick metal plate.

"I wonder how big this plate is?" he said to me.

He removed more dirt until he came to the end of the plate.

"It looks like a metal box or a safe. Holy crap, I found the money!" he exclaimed, wearing a big smile from temple to temple.

"What money?"

"The lost fortune. The money the old guy buried years ago when he lived in the 'big house.' Go tell mom! Tell her 'I' found the money!"

"Bursting with excitement, I ran as fast as my legs could take me. Reaching the back door, I flung open the screen door. It slammed against the house, putting a huge ding in the siding. *Dad's going to have a kitten when he sees his new paint job ruined.* Inside, I looked for Mom.

"Mom! Mom! We found the money!"

She was in the kitchen, busy cutting up apples to make an apple pie.

"What are you talking about?"

"The money, Mom! The hidden money!"

Mom's attention was focused on making the pie, not what I was saying. Finally, my great news sunk into her head.

"Where?"

"Over at Walter and Maryanne's house! Hurry, he's waiting to show you!"

It was the first time in my life I saw my mother run. She was the first to reach the screen door, throwing it open with so much force that it smashed into the house leaving even a bigger ding. *Dad's really going to have a fit when he sees two gashes in the wood!* We both ran to where my brother was standing, with his shovel stuck in the pile of dirt.

Proudly, he said, "After all these years, it took 'me' to find it!" Pointing down in the hole, he continued, "There it is, hidden for how many years?"

My mother looked at my brother with a warm, motherly smile and said, "You're going to share some of that money with your dad and me, aren't you?"

"I'm not sharing it with anyone—finder's keepers."

"Well, keep in mind, it's our property, not yours," my mother warned him.

"Walter, how about throwing a few bucks my way to buy parts to build crystal radios?" I pleaded.

"The first thing I'm buying is a good size fishing boat, one with a flying bridge and twin inboard engines. One that I can go a hundred miles off the coast to fish for tuna."

"After you give your dad and me our share," Mom reminded him. Bursting with excitement, she sprinted back to the house, and shouted with glee, "I've got to phone all our neighbors—tell them the good news!"

Walter was not happy about blabbing his discovery. In a desperate attempt to discourage her from calling neighbors, he facetiously yelled back, "You might as well call the *"Morristown Observer"* while you're at it."

"Great idea!" Mom shouted back as she neared the house.

Soon, many of our neighbors arrived, one after another. They stood around the hole, looking down at the metal box sealed with rusty screws. Everyone looked astonished at my brother's luck in finding the long-lost fortune. As they anticipated what treasure was inside the box.

My brother went back to the garage and came back with a large mallet and a cold chisel—a tool for cutting off rusty screws. He got down in the hole and labored to cut through the first large screw. Sweat dripped from his face as he worked away. After several minutes, he was through the first and had eleven more to go. He took his tee shirt off and started on the second.

An hour later, he had three more to go when I saw a strange car pull into my brother's driveway. The guy got out of the car and walked our way. A large camera hung from his neck. Reaching us, he announced, "Stan Wilson, *Morristown Observer.*"

My brother looked up at my mother and said, "Why did you do that? I was only kidding!"

He pulled out his notebook and pen and said to my mother, "What's this all about, finding a trove of hidden money?"

"It belonged to the guy that lived next door."

My mother continued telling it, all the details, all the mystery, how people have searched for years and never found it. Finally, here it was, in that black, rusty box. The reporter walked around the hole getting shots from many angles. Even one of my brother digging with his shovel.

He was down to the last screw and completely exhausted. He stood up supporting himself with the shovel. Another car came up the gravel driveway. I knew the sound well—my dad's car. The sound I heard when Dad caught my friends and I putting his favorite Jacobson lawn mower engine on our buggy. Dad parked his Chevy near the haunted barn and walked with a puzzled expression over to the crowd of neighbors huddled in our backyard. With great excitement and exuberance, my mother ran to him.

"Walter found the money! The money the wealthy guy in the 'big house' hid!"

Dad glanced down at the metal box in the hole, as my brother looked up at him, with a proud smile on his face.

"Here it is, I found it! I'm going to buy that fishing boat I always wanted!"

Dad began to laugh and said, "You may end up buying a rowboat—one with oars!"

The crowd of neighbors began to moan and complain amongst themselves about my dad's unexpected discouraging response.

"You know what you found? You found part of the septic system for this house."

Hearing that, the reporter, with a pissed-off expression, tore off the three pages of copious notes, crunching them in his hand, everything Mom had told him. He handed it to her and said, "Thanks a lot for the bogus story! I thought this was a front-pager, even had the title in my head, but ended up being a pile of shit!"

Chapter 15

My Body Was Going Crazy

Mendham Borough, NJ 1955

It was September in 1955 when I started 7th grade. That's when my body started going crazy. The first anomaly was the fuzz that started mysteriously growing all over my face. Each morning when I got up, I would look at myself in the mirror, shocked. It seemed that each day there was more fuzz. As an intellectual kid with an analytical mind, I thought. *God, at this rate, in a year, I'd look like a caveman!* I tried to ignore it and hoped that I wouldn't wake up one morning looking like a hairy gorilla.

Also, my voice got all weird sounding. It jumped from soprano to deep bass. If I tried to sing, my voice sounded horrible, everything off key. This became very evident when I attended church with my parents. When the organist played a hymn for the congregation to sing, everyone was in harmony with the music, except one person—me. Every time I sang, a few worshipers would look around our small congregation for the offending voice. It didn't take them long to stare right at me, which really upset me.

Being in a holy place of God, I had to be good. The Ten Commandments that I learned so well and memorized in Sunday school floated into my mind. It sort of flirted with my sense of good judgment, so I lip sang along. It was during the last hymn that I really wanted to join along and sing. It was a split decision in my mind; worship God and sing or keep peace and harmony in the congregation—to sing won. It only took one second before Mrs. Bockman, who sat in the pew in front of us, turned around and gave me a scowling look. At that moment, being good in church, for me, went right out the church window.

The next verse up I decided to let go of my secret weapon. I did just that and continued to sing with a big smile on my face. Everyone in our immediate area started to hold their noses.

Worshipers, near my family's pew, looked at one another trying to identify the guilty party, including my parents. Even Pastor Stearn, looked down at our pew in confusion, trying to figure out what was wrong.

My secret weapon must have been a doozy, because two pews down, Mrs. Elroy had elbowed her husband thinking he was the gassy one. Mr. Elroy, looked at his wife with an 'it wasn't me' expression.

God got even with me the very next day though. I walked into the music room and Miss Andrews immediately took me aside and said, "I don't think being in the choir is your thing."

"So, what you're telling me is, Miss Andrews, that I'm kicked out of the school choir."

"Don't think of it that way. Everyone has special talents and singing isn't one of yours."

"Thanks, Miss Andrews. I'll go back to building X-ray machines."

She looked back at me and said, "Really?" Then she quickly got back to the class to start practicing *God Bless America*. I sat in the back thinking about what next to build, waiting for the class to end.

Another odd thing that happened with my body was a driving interest in girls, especially, Annie. She was gorgeous, just like a young movie star, with long blond hair and dreamy blue eyes. She captured my attention all day in class. I looked at her unbelievable curves, her fair skin; *sugar and spice and everything nice* filled my mind.

At night, when I was asleep, my mind turned into a movie. All the films starred Annie, in living Technicolor. They played back everything that I had visualized of her during the day and even things that didn't happen. The sexiest one, the one I liked best, was Annie playing basketball in her athletic uniform—tee shirt and shorts. That one I played back repeatedly.

After eight hours of dreaming of Annie, I woke up in a weird physical state. I thought my mother should take me to see Dr. Hoffman. Something was seriously wrong with me.

I couldn't imagine going out in public in that state, especially school. But, after I jumped into the shower, which always started out cold before it warmed up, I returned to my old self again.

Annie was growing too, not only in height, but seemed to be getting curvier each day. While she was getting more girly, I was shooting up in height, the tallest guy in my class. My other friends expressed an interest in the opposite sex, too. *Sugar and spice and everything nice* rhyme went in circles in my head.

The fifties were puritanical times here in the United States. Sex education—absolutely none. Even saying the word sex meant a bar of Ivory soap in my mouth at home. My inquisitive mind wanted to know the secrets Annie unabashedly hid underneath her clothes. So, one afternoon, I headed for our living room library shelf and pulled out the 1945 edition, Encyclopedia of Britannica Index book. *What the hell was I going to look up? Was I going to look up women's breast? What she sported between her legs, I had no idea what they called it.* So, I started at A; it took me five minutes to read that one thin page. I quickly thumbed through the eight-hundred pages and mentally multiplied that by five minutes. Frustrated, I shoved the index back on the shelf.

After mulling over my plan of action, I decided to thumb through every volume. This would be an arduous task. It took forever to get through the first volume, but Annie was worth it. Flipping through the pages I noticed that the photos were poor quality, black and white; the drawings were even worse, very basic penned ones. Every day that followed, I was getting more frustrated thinking, *Britannica is even more censored than my mother.* Finally, I got to volume 'Z' and I thought that would be a useless place to find what sugar and spice Annie was made of. But, authors were a sneaky bunch, they liked playing tricks on you, putting the good stuff at the end of a book; just to make you read the entire book. *This probably applied to the Britannica too!* So, I charged forward and carefully checked out each page. My fingers were numb from all the page turning and my eyes were no better, bleary, all for the sake of Annie. I had gotten to the last page—nothing! In a fit of anger, I slammed the book shut and rammed it back on the shelf.

I learned more looking at the "National Geographic" than the entire Encyclopedia Britannica collection.

In grammar school, since I was a wiz at electronics, they chose me to be in the audio-visual group. We were in charge of running films on rainy days when kids couldn't go out for recess. The A-V teacher/advisor had me up on the stage playing John Philip Sousa Marches on an audio system with a record player whenever an activity or program was scheduled for the auditorium. I would have the machine blasting out *The Washington Post* march as each class entered the room and took their seats. When everyone was seated, I would adjust the audio for the teacher's introductory announcements.

For movies, we had a projection booth up on the second floor. We ran the movies up there using a sixteen-millimeter projector. Sometimes the film would break or a previous splice would snap. Kids absolutely loved when this happened—a detriment for the teachers. Teachers would go crazy trying to obtain order with over four hundred students smacking one another or shooting spit-balls. The din in the auditorium was like Yankee Stadium when Yogi Berra hit a home run.

It was a tense time for me to get the film repaired and loaded back into the projector. I would kill the lights in the auditorium, cross my fingers, and turn on the projector. Most often everything would be fine.

The auditorium was also a multipurpose room as well. At the beginning of the school year, we had our yearly physical health exam. Dr. Silvers was the chosen physician. His daughter, Dawn, happened to be in my class. Dr. Silvers would be stationed in one of our classrooms to examine all the boys.

It was Monday morning when Dr. Silvers started examining students. "Next. Stick your tongue out and say ah. Your parents need to do something about those tonsils. Unbutton your shirt," he told the next student.

It was my turn, he placed the cold stethoscope on my chest and listened. I wondered what he heard as my heart was beating like a woodpecker pecking on a tree. This was how the guys got their physicals. But the girls had a more private place for their examination—the auditorium.

When Dr. Silvers had finished his exams on the boys, it was the girls turn for the cold stethoscope. We were headed back to our classroom when Chris, also a seventh grader, ran up to me. He was also very talented with audio-visual equipment and was in our A-V group.

"Let's sneak into the booth and check out the girls. I've got the key, let's go," Chris said.

"Let's do it!" I said.

Once there, Chris put the key in the lock, and we stumbled into the dark booth. We closed the door and inched our way to the rectangular cut-out in the cement block wall.

"Where's Annie?" I whispered.

"She's back there, near the end of the line."

It was a Laurel & Hardy moment, as the two of us cracked our heads together trying to get a look at the girls.

Dr. Silvers was placing the stethoscope's diaphragm down Alice's blouse.

"Can't see a damn thing, his hand is in the way," I said.

Chris, being a jokester, whispered back, "I'll go down and tell him to get his damn hand out of the way—just for you, Greg."

The line was proceeding along with the doctor making notes on his clipboard after checking out each girl.

"Makes you want to be a doctor," Chris said.

"Na, rather be an engineer. Shhh, Annie is coming up next."

It had only taken a few moments for Annie's exam. "See Chris, she's perfect from head to toe. *Sugar and spice and everything nice.* Your idea of getting in the booth was great, but completely useless. I didn't learn a damn thing." As we made our way across the floor, my hand accidentally landed on the projector take-up reel, knocking it to the floor. It had hit with a loud clang that seemed to go on forever, echoing back and forth in the booth. Chris, cautiously looked out the projection hole from a distance.

"Dr. Silvers just removed his stethoscope from his ears and is looking up at the booth. We're fried!" Chris whispered.

We stood quietly, hearts pounding, waiting to see what he would do next. He continued to stare at the booth. The remaining girls looked up also and held their partially unbuttoned blouses tightly closed.

After what seemed an eternity, the doctor inserted the stethoscope into his ears and continued with the remaining exams. We snuck out of the booth and headed for our classroom.

Weeks and months went by as my nightly dreams starred with the blonde, blue-eyed Annie. But, that all changed when I was in high school and met Betty Lee in her red bathing suit on the beach at Barnegat Light, NJ. That was the summer I shared my first kiss with a girl—the one in the red bathing suit!

Chapter 16

RADIO 101

Mendham Borough, NJ 1952

My interest in radio began in fourth grade. I owe that interest to my Dad, Walter Lloyd Smith, who was born back in 1901 before the birth of broadcast radio, in the mid-twenties. Home crystal radio sets were common in the early part of the twentieth century. These radios could be bought commercially made, or constructed at home. Many companies sold crystal set kits that could be assembled in less than an hour. Some folks liked to experiment, building sets from parts bought at a local hardware store. Only a handful of parts were required; a Gallium crystal, a tuning coil assembly, a cat's whisker, a capacitor, copper wire, Fahnestock clips, and an earphone (headset). The radio was assembled on a small piece of wood using small wood screws.

Now and then, my dad would mention how he built crystal sets, not only for himself, but for friends and family. That sparked my interest in early radio when I was a fourth grader, I wanted to build one. One morning I popped the question to my dad. He was busy standing over the stove making pancakes.

"Dad, remember when you told me about those crystal sets you use to build?"

"Yeah, I do."

"Can we put one together?"

"Sure, but we'll need to get some parts. Ask your mom to save a cardboard oatmeal container, we'll need one before we can build a radio.'

"What do you need that for?"

"That's for the tuning coil, every radio needs one of those."

I found an empty cardboard oatmeal container and ran down to the basement. A few minutes later, Dad arrived and placed a bag of parts from the hardware store on the table. He pulled out the copper wire rolled on a wooden spool and the can of shellac from the bag.

"First you have to punch a hole at each end of the oatmeal container using a nail. After you do that, you have to wind the copper wire around the container, all the turns must be close together across the cardboard tube."

I had wound twenty turns, when the container slipped out of my left hand and all the wires unwound.

"You got to be more careful. I'll get something to keep the wire from unwinding."

Dad came back with some masking tape.

"Now, start winding the coil."

He applied the tape as I progressed winding the coil. I had over a hundred turns when I lost count. It took a zillion more turns to reach the end of the tube. Dad cut the wire and pushed the end through the hole.

Dad opened the shellac can, stirred it for a few minutes, and handed me a small paint brush.

"Put a nice even coat on all the wire. Try not to get any on your fingers. This will help keep the wire in place. Then, we'll let it dry overnight."

After coating the coil, I asked, "How's that Dad?"

"That's really good, let it dry overnight."

The following morning, I was raring to put the radio together. We were sitting around the kitchen table having breakfast when Mom killed those plans, "You better get dressed for Sunday school."

"But Mom, I want to stay here and work on the crystal set!"

"You heard your mother, you're going to Sunday school— end of discussion!"

"Dad, I feel sick. There's no way I can go."

"I guess you're too sick to work on the radio then," Dad retorted.

Well, I suddenly felt better and went to Sunday school.

After lunch, Dad went out to the ghost-ridden red barn to cut a board to build the radio. I ran down to the basement, bursting with excitement to finish our project. Later, Dad arrived with a piece of pine about a half inch thick, eight by ten inches. He began telling me step by step, how to fasten all the parts using little brass screws.

"The cat's whisker is next."

"That's a really strange name, why do they call it that?"

"Because it's a stiff wire with a little coil on it. The wire looks like a cat's whisker."

"Pretty funny if you ask me."

My dad pulled a small file out of his back pocket. I looked in horror as he filed off a strip of the pretty colored insulating enamel across the coil.

"Dad! What are you doing? You're ruining all my hard work!"

"We got to get to the bare wire. There's a tuning bar that needs to wipe along the coil to tune the radio."

Next, we mounted the Franstock clips for the antenna, ground, and headphones. These were made of spring brass and made electrical connections to the radio. You had to push down on the clip with one finger and insert the wire into the clip and then remove your finger. The spring tension would hold the wire and make an electrical connection.

"We have to make an antenna next." He handed me a hundred foot roll of wire and two glass insulators. "We'll need to string this from the house to a tree," Dad said.

Dad held the ladder while I attached the insulator and wire on a branch twenty feet up in the maple tree. We got to the house and installed the other insulator and strung-up the antenna. The antenna wire was then pushed through the cellar

111

window and connected to the crystal set. Dad connected the ground wire and the headphones.

I grabbed the headphones, placed them on my head and listened—nothing! No music, no news, absolutely nothing. I threw down the headphones on the table with great disappointment. "Dad, it doesn't work!"

"Just wait a minute—be patient. You have to find the active spot on the crystal."

"What do you mean by that?"

"You have to use the cat whisker on this small arm to poke around on the crystal. This will help you connect with a station."

"Well, that's a real pain in the ass," I said.

"Don't let your mother hear you say that word," Dad warned.

I put the headphones on and poked around the crystal, "Still nothing, Dad!" Almost ready to give up, I heard, "WMTR Morristown, a Sussex County man was arrested last night...."

"Do you have a station?"

"Dad—it works!

"This is how people listened to radio programs years ago. To be able to listen, everyone in the household had to be as quiet as a mouse. If two people wanted to listen, you had to share half the headset."

"This is really cool—no battery needed either. Thanks a million, Dad!"

"My dad and I shared one-half of the headset, one earpiece each, listening to WOR radio in New York City together, not saying a word, but proud of what we accomplished.

This paved the way for me to build tube radios and eventually get my FCC amateur radio license.

Chapter 17

Pirate Radio Station

Mendham Borough, NJ 1953-1954

After building dozens of crystal radios, my next childhood achievement, as a 6th grader, was to create a broadcast radio station. A few days before Christmas, I noticed a new present under the Christmas tree and the best part, it had my name on it. It was wrapped in red paper, covered in Santa's, each one seemed to wink at me. It may have been my imagination, but they seemed to tease me, saying, "Bet you can't guess what's in the box." After two days of noticing all those Santa's winking at me, I had to check out the present. The coast was clear; Mom and Dad were not around. I picked up the box to shake it, but found out it was too heavy, certainly not clothes for school—my least favorite present.

Finally, on Christmas morning, my dad had prepared a wonderful breakfast for us. Dad loved to make pancakes and sausage.

"May we open our presents first?" I shouted, standing in front of the tree.

"After breakfast," Dad shouted back.

We were waiting for Mom; she was taking forever to get out of bed. She wasn't a morning person. It took time, lots of time, to get her going. *Maybe I should bring her a strong cup of coffee.* Mom slowly walked to the kitchen, dressed in her light blue robe and slippers.

In a groggy voice, Mom exclaimed, "Merry Christmas!"

Dad and I enthusiastically replied, "Merry Christmas! Merry Christmas!"

Dad piled each one of our plates with a stack of delicious looking pancakes that he called flapjacks. A steamy aroma rose up from them that made our mouths water. I grabbed the maple syrup and generously poured it over mine until it flowed down over the edges. I had finished about half of them when my Dad asked if I wanted any more.

"No thanks, Dad. May I open my present, the one in the big, heavy box?"

"Sounds like you checked it out already. I'll bet you have no idea what's in the box."

"Not a clue, Dad!" *If I had my X-ray machine, the one Dr. Larson, unfortunately, destroyed; I would know exactly what was inside that box!*

"Oh, let him open it!" Mom said to Dad.

I didn't wait for Dad's answer. In a flash, I was ripping off the Santa Claus gift paper as Mom and Dad stood watching. There, on the side of the box, was a huge picture of an Allied Radio reel-to-reel tape recorder. I ripped open the box and struggled to lift the heavy machine out onto the carpet. It sparkled with newness and gave off an aroma, just like a new car. Thrilled with my present, I got up and hugged my parents.

"Thanks a million, Mom and Dad!"

"There're some blank tapes, too, somewhere," Dad said.

Just then, my private telephone rang. It had to be my friends, they were the only kids connected to it.

I ran to my bedroom to answer the phone. "Hello!"

"Merry Christmas, Greg! Guess what? We got an electronic lab set for Christmas! It has three vacuum tubes and a box full of electronic parts. You can make 100 different circuits! I can't wait for you to see it!" Al exclaimed.

"That sounds really neat, Al. I got a tape recorder!"

"What are you going to record?"

"I'm thinking of all the neat things to do with it. Maybe I'll play spy and secretly record a family holiday gathering. Record the conversations when the adults get talking about something controversial, especially after they have one or two cocktails. And if my brother is a bartender, it will be insane—he doubles up on the booze."

114

"That sounds really funny. I'll bet you'll get them started. You have a knack for doing that."

"You know it, buddy."

"Come over tomorrow and bring your soldering iron along with some solder and we'll build one of those electronic circuits, something really cool."

"Sure! See you tomorrow, Al!"

I ran back to the living room to continue exchanging gifts. I had to get those blank tapes. Not having any money to buy gifts, I made Mom a small bookshelf, to store her cookbooks and a tie holder for Dad. The last box I opened had the tapes. A big red stocking hung from the mantle, but I had already checked that out earlier while Dad was busy cooking.

Later that afternoon, relatives arrived to celebrate Christmas. Mom had prepared lots of goodies, she called them hors d'oeuvres, with a delicious dinner to follow. Dad had set up a bar with assorted drinks for the adults. After every one brought in their gifts and got seated, Mom and my sister, Wilma, passed around shrimp, stuffed celery, cheese, and crackers. My nephew, Steve, was there, too. He was five years younger, my best friend and like a younger brother to me.

We were sitting next to one another when I elbowed him and whispered, "My parents bought me a tape recorder. It's running, behind the green chair—recording everything."

"Do your parents know?"

"Nah—it's going to surprise the hell out of them when I play it back tomorrow."

"Your dad's going to blow a gasket! He might even confiscate the machine."

"I didn't think of that."

It was about an hour into the gathering when Walter and my father had gotten into a spirited discussion, more like an argument, about politics.

The controversy, as best I could tell, was over President Eisenhower criticizing McCarthy. Something about the Communists had infiltrated the Republican Party.

My brother fueled the fire when I heard him shout above the din, "Those damn Republicans, they're all a bunch of Communists!"

Dad, being a staunch Republican, stood up, pointed his finger at my brother, and said, even louder, "You're full of crap! As a Republican, you should know that's not true! Just a bunch of bull shit from those damn left-wing liberal Democrats—they're all a bunch of Communists, rewarding people for not working, sitting on their asses, and collecting welfare checks. They're turning this country into a welfare state."

"Who said I was a Republican?" my brother yelled back.

"What do you mean, you're not a Republican? You're a Democrat?"

"You're damn tooting I am!"

"Give me strength! Well, the next time this country goes to war, remember who you voted for!" Dad shouted back.

With loose tongues, the heated political debate flew insults back and forth with no winners; just two opinionated personalities. I smiled knowing every word and insult was going on tape. *This is so wild! Can't get any better! I don't think I can play it back to them, it will just get them going again—get me in trouble, for sure.*

The next day I had gone to my friends' house with my soldering equipment to see their electronics lab. It was cool, all new components, including three radio tubes. The lab was powered by household power, so you didn't need expensive batteries. I thumbed through the project book, 100 projects. All the great things you could build fascinated me. You could even build a broadcast radio transmitter. I sat there on the floor reading the instructions.

"I think we should build this project, guys. We'll have our own radio station, right here in Mendham!

Can you imagine how exciting that could be? We could play music, give weather information, and tell all the school news."

"Sounds pretty exciting to me, but drop the weather stuff. That's stupid, people just have to look out their windows for that," Sam said.

We plugged in the soldering iron and began building the radio transmitter. We spent almost the entire day wiring all the parts together and finished the last step, plugging in the three tubes.

"Who's going to be the brave one to plug it in?" questioned, Al.

"I'll do it," answered Sam as he plugged it into the outlet.

"Passed the smoke test, nothing caught on fire!" I commented.

The tubes lit up with a warm yellow-orange glow.

"Turn your radio on; set the dial for no stations. Al went over to his table radio, turned it on, and adjusted the tuning dial. I turned the radio transmitter, tuning until I heard a loud hiss on his radio. I then picked up the microphone, and talked into it, "This is radio station B—L—A—B hidden somewhere in Mendham."

"Give me the mic," Sam commanded. "The Martians have landed in Mendham and have taken over the public school. The police chief tried to stop them, but was taken prisoner."

I grabbed the mic away. "Sam, you idiot! You'll have the State Police and the National Guard searching for us!"

The instructions read; Warning! Only use a ten-foot piece of wire for an antenna to limit range pursuant to FCC regulations (Federal Communications Commission). I looked at Al and Sam with a smile on my face. "We could hook this to my 200-foot long wire antenna. I'll bet this baby will really get out, transmit all over town! We could test the distance if we had a portable radio." Unfortunately, none of us had one.

Note: Portable radios of that era used miniature vacuum tubes, often referred to as peanut tubes. They required two

*batteries; A & B. The 'A' battery was 1&1/2 volts and the 'B'
either 67 or 90 volts.*

"I got an idea, guys. Tomorrow I'll take my Radio Flyer
wagon down to the Chevy dealer and see what I can find in
their scrap heap. We can use a car radio for the test," I
suggested.

"Lots of luck with that," Sam said, in a not so promising
voice.

The next day I got ready to go to the Chevy dealer. It had
snowed that night. I put my coat and boots on and went to the
red barn to get my wagon. I was in and out before the ghost
saw me. *Probably still sleeping after a night of haunting.* I
trudged through the snow, through my friends' yard, down
Main Street to the car dealership. Most customers went to the
front of the building to do their business, but I went to the
back, where all the free stuff was. There in the back, near the
junk pile, was an old Chevy sedan, smashed-up from a bad
accident, covered in snow, ready to be towed away. I walked
into the service department to see Louie. Louie treated me
well; he knew my parents and the Gunthers were good friends.

"Louie, I need to get a car radio, battery, and antenna.
There's a wreck out back, ready to go to the junkyard, may I
strip those parts out of it?" I asked him.

"The insurance company is towing it out today; did you
bring any tools with you?"

"No, I don't have any."

"See Andy, he'll lend you what you need. Be careful with
the battery, it has sulfuric acid in it, that can burn your skin
off."

It took me almost an hour to remove the parts. I had just
removed the antenna when the wrecker arrived. The guy
backed his tow truck to the wreck and fastened the tow cable.
He looked at me and the parts in the wagon.

"I didn't see a thing," he said, as he winched the front of the
car above the ground.

With the heavy battery loaded, I struggled to pull the wagon over the snow-covered sidewalk to get home. I couldn't believe my luck, finding everything I needed.

Down in the lab, I connected the speaker and antenna. I wired the radio to the car battery, crossed my fingers, and turned on the radio. It buzzed and the dial light came on, but not a sound. These radios used tubes and you had to wait a minute or two until they warmed-up—still nothing! I jiggled the antenna plug and WABC came blasting out the speaker with the number one song of the week, *"Love You, Baby."*

Around ten in the morning the next day, my friends arrived at my house. Al carried the transmitter and Sam brought the microphone. We connected the mic and antenna, then plugged it in. The tubes slowly lit.

"Shhhh—anything you say will be broadcasted," I whispered.

"Somebody has to stay here and talk continuously into the mic, so we can test it."

"It's not going to be me, too boring," Al said.

"Not me either. I want to be where the action is," Sam added.

"This is my idea and I'm not staying here talking my head off, for God knows how long. We need some audio that can be on all the time, like a buzzer or bell."

"Your parents aren't going to like that," Sam commented.

"I got it! We can wire the tape recorder directly to the transmitter. It will be completely silent," I said.

We wired the recorder to the transmitter and started the tape; it would run for a good hour. Wearing our coats and gloves, we went outside to the wagon and turned on the radio. Our Christmas day family celebration was being transmitted, loud, and clear.

Off we went, taking turns pulling the wagon. We had gotten about a mile down the sidewalk on Main Street with great radio reception, when my dad's voice came screaming out of the speaker, "You're full of crap!"

The twins looked at me and said, "Was that your father?"

"Yup, that's him alright. My brother spiked his drink! He'll get kind of crazy and say exactly what's on his mind."

The hot political rant continued. Then, I realized the whole town of Mendham might be listening! There was no way to stop it. We were too far away. Dad and my brother were screaming back and forth.

"We got to shut that damn thing off! Dad is going to be so pissed, if he finds out we're transmitting our family business all over town, we are all going to get in trouble."

"Well, it was your idea to use the tape recorder," replied Al.

"No sense of busting our asses to get home, the tape will end by the time we get back." *This is a small town; I'm sure only a few people who changed stations, landed on Mendham's radio station, B L A B!*

We headed back, much less enthused then we started. We turned onto Hillcrest Rd., then again to the Smith clan up on Hillcrest Place. Al was the first to see my dad sitting on his Farmall tractor, plowing the four inches of snow that had fallen last night. He stopped in front of us and looked down in the wagon.

"What are you guys up to now? Aren't you a little old for playing with a wagon?"

"We had to move this heavy car battery over to Al and Sam's house, just returning to do another experiment in the lab. Next time, I'll use your tractor, Dad!"

"You will not! Keep using the wagon, you can't get into any trouble using that."

You have no cotton picken' idea, Dad.

We got out of his way, as Dad put the Farmall in gear and continued to plow.

I kept my hopes up that no one had heard our radio broadcast.

The next morning Mom, Dad, and I headed for Hilltop Church. We got there a little early; Mom and Dad bowed their heads in prayer, as they always did. I glanced over to the other side of the church and saw Mr. Abbott get up and walk toward us with a big smile on his face. After Dad finished his prayer, Mr. Abbott tapped him on the shoulder.

"That was one doozy of a Christmas party you had!"

"What do you mean, Elmer? How would you know?"

"Your family party was broadcasted over radio station B L A B yesterday. We especially enjoyed the political part, the part about your son being a Democrat—living in your household, no less! Right under your nose! You never knew it! Every time you voted Republican, he voted Democrat. He canceled out every one of your votes!"

Mr. Abbott broke out laughing and Dad looked like he was ready for a heart attack, sitting there in the pew, speechless, white as a sheet.

"I wouldn't be surprised that half the town heard your Christmas celebration. As the saying goes, you never know what goes on behind closed doors. You guys were better than any radio program I've heard in a long time."

"Jan, we're going home now to sort this mess out," my dad grumbled, in my mother's ear.

Dad grabbed me by suit jacket collar and pulled me out of the pew. As the congregation piled in the church, we piled out, all three of us! Several church members glanced at us in confusion as my Dad whisked me out of the church.

We got in the car and Dad slammed his door shut, he was upset, too upset to drive. He turned to me and said, "This has all the markings of something that you would do. When we get home, I'm boxing up that damn tape recorder. Can you imagine, Jan? Half the town might have heard this!"

"When will I get it back, Dad?"

121

"Not anytime soon, but if you do, there will be absolutely no recordings of family events."

Just as we were ready to leave, Mr. Anderson knocked on my dad's car window. Dad rolled it down with the crank handle.

"Next year, my wife and I are going to your house for Christmas! You guys were a riot, better than any radio comedy! Merry Christmas! See you all next Christmas!"

Chapter 18

Quiet Hours!

Mendham Borough, NJ 1955

This is my story on how I became a radio amateur (Ham). I have served the communities of Mendham, Morris Plains, and Chatham in emergency radio communications. I currently hold an FCC Extra Class Radio License, call sign, W2GLS.

Mendham's one and only test broadcast station, BLAB was short-lived, it was only on the air for less than one hour. With my friends borrowed broadcast transmitter gone and my Christmas present, the tape recorder, packed-up, ready to be shipped back to Allied Radio, station BLAB was shut down for good. The momentary fun of running our illegal pirate broadcast station inspired me to obtain a legal station license, an FCC (Federal Communications Commission) Novice Class license. It would require me to pass a Morse code test and written examination.

Other than knowing SOS in Morse code (... --- ...) by heart as a young Cub Scout, I had no clue what the other codes were. I sent for the *ARRL (American Radio Relay League) License Manual* by mail. Two weeks later, it arrived and I started my arduous study, learning three letters each day. My fellow classmates thought I had gone weird, seeing me drawing little dots and dashes all over my brown paper bag book covers. I had gotten halfway through the alphabet, L,M,N, when I noticed Mr. Johnson, our teacher, standing alongside my desk observing my hieroglyphics.

"What kind of nonsense are you scribbling on your book cover?"

Caught red-handed I was forced to spit out the truth, "Morse code, Mr. Johnson."

"I'll bet you didn't hear one word I said for the last half-hour."

"No, it sort of went in one ear and out the other."

"Plan to stay after school for a replay. Put those books on the floor and pay attention!"

The first week of school and I'm already in for detention. Mom and Dad will be thrilled!

Over the next two weeks, I worked on memorizing the dots and dashes for the entire alphabet, numbers, and a few symbols. I thought I was pretty darn clever using it to respond to my parents. Especially when they told me to do something I wasn't inspired to do or something that I forgot to do. My mother thought it was cute, even chuckled; but Dad, not so much, especially after he tripped on several of my wires draped across the tiles down in the basement, in my laboratory.

Stunned, Dad said, "For God's sake why would you run wires running in front of the bottom step?"

Without thinking, I replied, "Well, I knew they were there!"

Dad got up and said, "Get a wire-cutter and get them out of here—NOW!"

"Dit dah, dit dah, dit dah," I mouthed, out loud.

"Stop being a wise guy, with that code stuff."

"Why, Dad? Mom and you talk Dutch whenever you don't want me to know something."

"We're the parents and you are our son—we make the rules!

Rule number 126, no more smart-ass Morse code responses.

With my memorized knowledge of Morse code, I turned on my shortwave radio to listen to the ARRL code practice session at 7:00 pm. Wearing my headset, I listened intently as they sent code at a rate of five words per minute, picking up an 'A' now and then. This was turning out to be more difficult than I had anticipated. Knowing the dots and dashes and the sound of them being sent was very different. Week after week, I continued to practice, learning the sound of more letters. A month later, I reached a milepost, I copied a complete word.

A few weeks later, I was printing out almost every word and number the ARRL sent from their station W1AW at Newington, Connecticut.

Now I had to practice sending code. Not having a sending key, I made one, by first cutting a half-inch strip of metal from a soup can with tin snips and mounting it on a wooden board with a woodscrew. I used a second screw for the mating contact. With wires connected to each screw, the telegraph key was set to go, except for the insulated sending knob. Then it dawned on me. In a couple of minutes, Mom and Dad's toothpaste cap was glued to the metal strip with Duco cement.

Having a good grasp of the code, I started learning all the required stuff the FCC wanted a licensee to know; electronic symbols, circuits, operating frequencies, and regulations. I was motivated, every spare moment, studying the license manual.

To take the Novice test, I needed a General Class licensed radio amateur to administer it. Bob, who also lived in Mendham and attended high school, had a General. He was really nice and enthused, just like me, with radio communications. He introduced me to a Chicago based company, Allied Radio, the previous summer; they sold electronic parts and kits. After I received their catalog, my eyes zeroed in on a Philmore one-tube radio kit. That evening, my piggy bank went empty to finance the kit that Bob graciously ordered for me.

The next day, after school, I gave Bob the money for the kit. I told him that I had studied for the test and practiced Morse code each night, listening to W1AW, and that I was ready to take the FCC test. He sent a letter to the FCC requesting the Novice test.

Two weeks later, we met after school, in a classroom, Bob placed a *QST*, a magazine for radio operators, on my desk.

"Pick a page," he said.

I flipped through the pages like a card dealer and landed on page 73. "Page 73, Bob."

"That's a number you'll be using often. Okay, let me send a couple of sentences from that page for practice, then we'll begin the official code test."

I grabbed my pencil and paper. I was nervous. Bob started sending Morse code and I printed on paper what he was sending. After the second sentence he sent; dit da, dit da, dit da—the code for a period or full stop.

After completing the code test, Bob told me I passed and handed me the test pamphlet. There were only twenty questions and it took me less than one-half hour to complete. I checked each question twice, making sure I didn't mess up. With my fingers crossed, I handed the test booklet and answer sheet back to Bob. He glanced down at my answers.

"Congratulation! You've passed!"

I took a deep breath and vigorously shook Bob's hand.

For weeks, I had checked our mailbox each day at the US Post Office next to the grammar school—no license. I had almost given up when I removed the business-sized envelope from our box with the FCC return address. Trembling, I slit the envelope open with my index finger and viewed my station license, call sign—WV2NAV. *I'm legally licensed! This is the most exciting day of my life!*

After arriving home, I ran around the house to find Mom to tell her the world breaking news.

"Station BLAB was gone forever, but WV2NAV will be blasting through the universe for years to come!" I hurried to my room to make my first broadcast. A few minutes later, after my radio warmed up, numerous code stations beeping away out of the speaker. My two-tube transmitter lit up, tubes glowing a bright yellow-orange color. I held the key down and the transmitting vacuum tube glowed blue as it pumped out continuous radio waves at a frequency of 3710 kilohertz. With my free hand, I placed my neon electrical tester near the antenna wire. Like magic, it lit up without touching anything!

I started tapping out 'CQ' in Morse code, inviting any radio station to chat with me. Novice station KN3BUV responded back. We exchanged our names, where we lived, signal reports, and our radio equipment along with the type of antenna. I said goodbye to Jerry, who lived in Pittsburg, Pennsylvania by sending two digits, 73, a shortcut in code. I logged him into my station logbook. Before Mom called me for dinner, I was able to contact three more stations!

After dinner, Dad went to the family room to watch TV on our small screen black and white set and I split for my room to transmit.

Dragnet was on, I could just about hear the TV from my room, Sergeant Joe Friday was interviewing a witness to a crime. "The facts mam, nothing but the facts," he said. After my equipment warmed-up, I wanted to check to see if my transmitter was working and pushed down the key. To my surprise, I heard the voice of Sargent Friday completely disappear and a loud buzz took its place over the TV. *Was that me?* I let up the key and the buzz stopped, Sargent Joe started talking again.

"What in the world happened to the TV?" Dad asked.

I started sending some Morse code and I could hear the TV sputter and buzz in sync with each of my dots and dashes.

"Is that you interfering with my TV?" Dad shouted from the family room.

"No Dad," I shouted back.

"I started sending out CQ's to find a station to contact." I could hear Dad's TV going crazy.

"Are you sure? The picture is flipping, rolling, and the sound is a loud buzz that goes on and off," Dad shouted.

I wanted to log in more stations and stay on the air. Knowing my dad, the great detective would soon discover I was the one responsible. *What could I do to trick him? Maybe, set a book on the key so the transmitter is sending all the time. Then walk into the family room so he sees me. That might convince him.*

With my math book on the key, I arrived in the family room. Joe Friday had disappeared from the TV. Large black bar images were rolling up the screen, like train tracks.

127

The buzzing was so loud and disturbing that I had to put my hands over my ears.

"See Dad, it's not me. It must be your set; you probably need a new one."

"It was working just fine. It's probably some damn kid with a CB (citizen band) radio! Wait till tomorrow, I'm going to call the FCC and file an interference complaint.

Oh, crap!

Dad shut the TV set off and grabbed a book to read while I went back to my bedroom. The transmitting tube plate (element) was cherry red—super hot. It looked like I was going to have a thermal meltdown situation in my bedroom

After the tube cooled down, I went back on my merry way, sending CQ's and contacting more stations in bordering states. Then I heard a prefix, W8, which had to be further away, perhaps Ohio or Kentucky! In deep concentration, with my hand on the sending key, and my other hand on the antenna switch, I was ready to land the station. While being entirely focused on W8FTL, I never heard my bedroom door open. An angry figure stood quietly watching—my dad. I held my breath; the station was ready to listen for responding stations, as he sent 'K.' Then it happened without warning, the overhead light went out; the room went into total darkness. *Did I blow a fuse? No, the tubes were still lit on my radio equipment.*

Seconds later, the light came back on and there was Dad, standing in my doorway with his hand on the light switch.

"I don't have to call the FCC, I know exactly 'who' is knocking out my TV."

"You need to get a filter for your TV, Dad."

"You need to be off the air and doing your homework."

"But Dad! I just got my license today! I've waited all my life for this moment, to be on the air. I was even pretending to be Samuel Morse!"

"You need to be Greg Smith, doing his homework. Another thing, if you're killing my TV, I'll bet you're interfering with

128

our neighbors as well. I'm going to limit when you can use that transmitter."

Here comes rule number 102.

"You can only transmit during 'quiet hours' when no one is watching TV. There's one more stipulation, only after your homework is done, and checked."

The next day, I waited for the old 1948 Chevy bus to drop-off students coming back from Morristown High School. Bob got off the bus with a stack of books under his arm. I ran over to him. "I got my license, WV2NAV."

"Did you make your first contact?"

"I made a string of them! That came to a screeching halt though when I killed *Dragnet* on TV."

"You need to use an RF filter and put a metal shield over your transmitter."

"Like it was radio-active?"

"Same idea."

I was not able to solve the problem of knocking out TV reception in our neighborhood. So, I had to restrict my use of the station to the early morning, afternoon, and late at night when Mom and Dad were fast asleep. One night I got the idea to see who I could reach at midnight. *The only one up at that time is usually the ghost that resides in the red barn.* I set Little Ben for 12 and fell asleep. At midnight, the clock went off. I switched on the light and turned my equipment on. Still half asleep, with my headphones on I, heard stations with a 6 prefix—California! WOW! *Coast to coast! All the way across America!*

Station WN6FOX was calling CQ, then signed, sending PSE K (please respond). I replied using my station call sign, WV2NAV. He sent back, QRZ (please repeat). I repeated WV2NAV three times. He sent, WV2NAV de (this is) WN6FOX. My heart beat rapidly. My little homemade transmitter had sent a radio signal across the country.

Chapter 19

The TV Repair Kid

Mendham Borough, NJ 1956

Home entertainment took a big jump when DuMont announced home television. The first models had ten-inch round picture tubes. Adults enjoyed shows like *Milton Berle, Bob Hope*, and even shoot-um-up cowboy shows. Kids were glued to shows like *Howdy-Doody* and *Kukla, Fran, and Ollie*. They all appeared in black and white.

Television antennas popped-up on rooftops like quills on a porcupine. At some homes, people had two antennas pointing to different cities to get double the channels.

TV repair shops popped up across the country. Most offered in-home service and drop-off service at the shop. With steel chassis and wood cabinets, these sets were hernia makers, discouraging most folks from bringing the sets into the shop for service. They were willing to pay extra for in-home repair.

Early TV, used vacuum tube technology that required lots of power and created lots of heat. The tubes deteriorated each time the TV was turned on and sometimes died of premature death. This fact was a goldmine for servicemen.

Back then, in my early teens, I was in an electronics learning loop—read, learn, and experiment. Every broken radio was a challenge to find what components failed. I was an electronics detective, checking for what didn't work, visual inspection of burnt up components, and odd-ball voltages. I couldn't afford to buy a test meter with a 35-cent weekly allowance, so I built one from Bell Labs junk I bought at a Morristown junkyard—Winarsky's. My success at repairs was pretty good, especially for a kid.

When TV first came out, there was little published on its technology and how it worked—it was a secret!

DuMont and RCA kept it close to their chest. They wanted to keep it a secret from other companies.

TV repair was lethal with 20, 000 to 30, 000 volts looming inside each cabinet. That discouraged homeowners to be do-it-yourselfers, pulling the tubes and have them tested. The exception was electrical engineers and radio amateurs.

Servicemen were quite good at their trade, seeing the problem, pulling the bad tube, and replacing it with a tube from their tube caddies. The tube caddy was like a tube store in a case. The black case flipped open holding dozens of tubes. Many of the tube boxes were worn, causing customers to wonder if they got second-hand tubes from someone else's TV.

It was a sweltering Saturday, mid-August afternoon, and my dad was glued to the TV watching the New York Yankees play the Brooklyn Dodgers—rival teams. The Dodgers were up with two men on bases as Jackie Robinson stepped up to the batting plate. Whitey Ford threw a curveball that eluded Robinson's bat. Strike, signaled the umpire. The Yankee fans stood and roared shouting, "Go Yankees! Go Yankees!" Yogi Berra returned the ball and the TV picture started to roll up and off the screen.

Dad, yelled, "It never fails when things get exciting."

He got up out of his chair, twiddled with the vertical hold knob, and by the time he got back to his chair the picture was rolling so fast it turned into a blur.

"Damn! I guess I'll have to turn on the radio—that works all the time," he blurted out.

The magic word didn't seem to work on the TV. "Want me to fix it, Dad?"

"Since when did you know anything about fixing a TV?"

"Can't be that hard, look at all the radios I have fixed."

"You're not going to kill yourself going inside that set, are you?"

"Nope. I watched that TV repair guy that came here a few months ago. I asked him so many questions that he asked me if

I wanted to be a TV repairman when I grow up. I told him no, I want to do it now and be a TV repair kid."

Dad watched closely as I removed the antenna cable and removed the back panel on the TV. I looked at the tube diagram inside the set and found the location of the vertical hold tube. I went to the kitchen and came back with a dish towel.

"There's high voltage in there," Dad warned.

"I'll be careful; I'll stay away from the high voltage so I don't get zapped," as I pulled the tube.

"We better get to Robinsons Drug Store before it closes," Dad, suggested.

I held the hot tube in the dish towel as we piled into the car for Robinsons. They had a floor standing tube tester in the back of the store. The bottom portion held replacement tubes. I set the switches and placed the tube in the socket. As the tube lit up, the big panel meter needle moved into to the red scale, indicating 'BAD.' I grabbed a replacement boxed tube from the storage area below and gave it to Dad for him to pay for.

Fifteen minutes later at home, I plugged in the new tube.

"Are you sure this is going to work?" Dad asked.

Five minutes later, the game came on and Dad was thrilled, almost. The Yankees were winning by a landslide and he was an avid Dodgers fan.

The news of my acquired talent traveled fast to my much older brother and sister who married and lived close by. As their TV's died, I took over repairing them, as well. The news must have spread on our telephone party-line because neighbors started calling Mom and Dad for the TV repair kid to fix their sets, too. Since money was scarce and people needed to be thrifty, they welcomed me with open arms. Some, offered me a cookie or two after I got their TV working, never any bills.

To diagnose the TV, I had to ask, "What's wrong with the TV?" I needed an accurate answer, like no sound, completely dead or no picture. Sometimes the neighbor would just say,

"It doesn't work." That would require me to turn on the TV, to see for myself. Doing that turned the TV into an execution box since the lethal voltage would be present for hours. If it was a high voltage problem, I had to come back the next day when the high voltage discharged.

I had just gotten home from school and headed into the house for a snack.

"How was school today?" Mom asked.

"Baking! So hot, that the nurse handed out salt tablets! Five minutes later, the whole class shot out the door fighting each other for a drink at the water fountain, including the teacher! We no sooner got back to our desks, when we got thirsty again and headed back to the fountain."

"What kind of subjects are you studying?" Mom asked.

"Pre-algebra, for one. Most of the kids really got confused about solving for X. We had enough of a problem coming up with the right answer with numbers—adding X to the mix now, put us back to square one."

"Well, did you understand the concept using X?"

"Confusing. I still have X's bouncing back and forth in my brain."

"How about a root beer float, that will make you feel better?"

"I can go for that."

Just as Mom walked toward the refrigerator, the black telephone on the wall rang. Mom picked it up.

"Oh hi, Diane. Yeah, he just arrived home. I'm sure he won't mind. I'll send him over after he has his float."

"That was Mrs. Lenard over on Orchard Street. She asked if you could look at their TV, it went on the fritz this morning."

"Sure thing, Mom. As soon as I finish this float.

I had my spoon in the glass trying to get at the ice cream. Every time I went to dig a spoon into the ice cream, it dove like a submarine to the bottom. After a few swallows, I solved that problem.

In my bedroom, under my bed, I grabbed my small metal toolbox and the old belt hanging on a nail in my closet—the one I had outgrown. My toolbox had everything I needed to get inside a TV. Outside, I strapped my toolbox to the metal rack, fastened behind the seat, on my bike. This should be a piece of cake to fix Mrs. Lenard's TV, she lived right around the block on Orchard Street. Ten minutes later, I was removing the toolbox and she was at the door inviting me in.

"Hi Mrs. Lenard, Mom told me your TV quit on you."

"Hi, Greg. Yes, that's right. It's really nice of you to help us out. Nothing works on the TV; no sound or picture, just a blank gray screen."

"In the house, I walked over to the RCA TV sitting on a floor stand. Can you help me lift this TV stand around?"

"Sure."

"She sat in a chair across from me and watched as I got a tool and removed the back of the TV. I pulled my cheater cord out of the toolbox, to power-up the set."

"What's that?"

"It's a cheater cord. It allows me to run the TV without the back on."

"You be careful!"

I plugged the cord in and turned on the TV—nothing. *Dead as a doornail, as dad would say.* I looked at each tube to make certain all were lit. *Ah, the 5U4G rectifier tube is as dark as night.* "It's the rectifier tube, Mrs. Lenard."

"Where can we get a new one?"

"Robinsons, uptown. Give me five bills and I'll bring back the change. With five singles in my pocket, I took off on my bike, past Gunther Motors, up the hill to Robinsons."

Dr. Robinson, the pharmacist, was standing behind the drug counter filling prescriptions. He glanced over at me coming through the front door, heading his way for the tube tester.

"Testing another tube, Greg?"

"Not this time, I know which one is bad."

"You're our best tube customer we have here."

"Being the TV repair kid, I need to buy lots of tubes, Dr. Robinson."

I pulled the 5U4G boxed tube from the cabinet under the tester, paid for it and headed out the door. Coasting down the hill, I was at the Lenard's home in no time. I rang the bell and Mrs. Lenard came to the door.

"That was fast!" she said.

I plugged in the tube and turned the set on. The set hummed for a couple of minutes and then came alive with three cowboys shooting at a Wells Fargo stagecoach—POW! POW! POW!

"Oh! Oh! It works!" she screamed. "You're such a wiz at fixing TV's".

"That's why people call me the TV Repair Kid, Mrs. Lenard."

I gave her the change from my pocket and fastened the back onto the TV. A few minutes later, we jockeyed the set back to where it was. My face was still burning up, as sweat dripped down from my forehead from biking to Robinsons.

"How about a nice cold Coke?" Mrs. Lenard asked.

"Sounds good to me."

Back from the refrigerator, she handed me a frosty glass bottle of Coke. I gulped a few swallows and put the glass against my forehead to cool me down.

After finishing the Coke, I went outside to fasten the toolbox, hopped on my bike, and headed home.

The TV repair kid did it again! That was one piece of cake to get that RCA TV running.

I just got in the door, ready to watch that same cowboy program, when Mom caught me on my way to our TV.

"Mrs. Stephens called, she needs her TV repaired; she would appreciate it if you would look at it. She promised her husband that she would get it fixed today. All the service people she called, told her next week was the soonest they could come out."

"I'm kind of tired Mom after fixing the Lenard's TV."

"I promised her you'd look at it."

"What does she mean by looking at it? That always gets me, when people say that to me. One of these days I'm just going to do that. Walk into someone's living room, look at the TV, and say, "Yup, it isn't working," then walk right out the door."

"Stop being so cross! See if you can get it going for them. She mentioned that Hans will go crazy if he can't watch his ball game on Saturday."

Fortunately, the toolbox was still strapped to my bike. I hopped on it, for the short ride, about two blocks away. I kicked the bike stand down, went to the door, and rang the bell.

As the door opened, Mrs. Stephens, in bare feet, wearing shorts and a tee, was straining to hold, Bowser, her German Sheppard, back by the collar, as he growled and barked at me. "Shut-up Bowser! Hi Greg, thanks so much for coming over to look at our TV. Let me pull him back so you can come in."

"Are you sure it's safe, Mrs. Stephens?"

"He's harmless, just makes a lot of noise at strangers."

She pulled him back and I placed my foot inside, Bowser showed his teeth and growled at me again. "Bowser—shut-up!" She commanded.

I gave the dog wide birth, as I walked over to the large wood console TV in the living room, decorated with pink flowered, green wallpaper. I wasn't in the greatest mood, from the heat of the day, along with Algebra still banging around inside my head. *Should I just look at it, say yup, it's not working, and leave.* "What's wrong with your TV, Mrs. Stephens?"

She glanced at me, still holding the dog, with a strange look on her face and says, "It's not working—like I told your mother."

"Is there any sound? Is there a picture? Or neither?" I asked.

"Oh yes, the sound works just fine, but no picture."

"It's probably the vertical output tube in the high voltage cage. When was the last time the set was turned on?"

"I tried it again this morning and still no picture."

"The TV probably has some high voltage still stored inside. It's drained down though, but can give you a nasty jolt. I can come back tomorrow when it will be completely discharged."

"Hans's going to be really upset with me when he gets home if I don't have this fixed."

"Okay, I'll really need to be careful," as I swung the TV away from the wall and removed the back. I located the high voltage cage and removed the cover. As I looked inside, I saw all the high voltage parts that could electrocute me, if high voltage was present." *Is it worth two cookies to get myself killed? Not really.* I saw the tube I needed to pull with the high voltage wire on top. I stuck my arm in the cage to remove it, startled the dog, and two seconds later, he's on my back pushing my arm further into the cage—I'm getting shocked like hell with my body convulsing!

"Get off of him, Bowser!" She screamed, over and over.

Mrs. Stephens struggled to get the dog off. Finally, she mustered enough strength to pull both the dog and me away from the TV, with me falling backward on top of the dog. I can feel his hot breath on my neck as he continued to attack me. I rolled over with him now on top of me forcing me to sprawl flat against the carpet.

Jaws still clamped to my shirt, I felt the dog's claws digging into my skin. His front feet slid down my back, opening my skin like a razor with his sharp claws.

"Bowser let go! Bad Bowser! Bad dog!" She screamed. She grabbed his collar with both hands and pulled him off. She struggled to get him into the bathroom to lock him up. Mrs. Stephens, came back running to me, to see if I was okay, as the dog barked like crazy and raked the door with all his might trying to get at me.

"Did he bite you? Let me check. No bite marks, that I can see. You got some pretty good size open wounds on your back from his claws though. Let me fix you up with some iodine and band-aids." She eased open the bathroom door with the dog still going crazy, slipping through, she got the stuff.

"Take your shirt off, what's left of it, and I'll bandage you up." She dabbed the iodine on, as I gave up trying to be a man—and yelled: "OW!"

"Sorry, that stung. I need to put the iodine on the rest of the wounds."

A half hour later, I parked my bicycle in front of Robinsons Drug Store. The place was crowded with people that had come from work picking up newspapers, medicine, and everything else. As I walked into the store with what was left of my shirt, everyone was looking at me in horror. Dr. Robinson, the pharmacist, came running over to me.

"What in God's name happened to you, Greg? Did some kid beat you up? You must have fifteen band aides on your back! Your shirt is ripped to shreds! Are you okay? Want me to call the squad?"

"A big German Sheppard beat the crap out of me," I responded.

"You better make sure that dog's up to date with vaccinations."

I pulled out the boxed tube, put my hand in my pocket—no money. *She forgot to give me the damn money!* I was ready to put the tube back when Dr. Robinson motioned to me to see him.

"Give me the tube," he said, as he slipped it into a prescription bag. He scribbled the price on the outside of the bag. "Pay me later."

"Thanks, Dr. Robinson, I'll get the money to you tomorrow."

I got back to the Stephens's house and rang the bell.

"You look terrible! Your shirt is ruined. I'm so, so sorry. Come on in."

"I'm not coming in until that dog is locked up, preferably in a cage."

"He's locked down in the basement. He made a mess out of the bathroom door—Hans will be furious when he sees what condition the door's in."

"I fixed the TV and gave the bag to Mrs. Stephens to pay Dr. Robinson. Then biked home, Dad was watching the news, having an evening cocktail, and Mom was in the kitchen preparing dinner.

"Oh my God! What happened to you? Look at your shirt, it's in threads!" Mom blurted out with fear marked all over her face.

"Bowser pushed me inside her TV and I got shocked to hell!" I yelled.

Hearing that, my father came running in from the den to see what condition I was in.

"Well, I'm calling her right now! What's wrong with her? Leaving her dog unattended, so he can bite the crap out of you!"

"Dad, she was holding him and he got away," I said.

Dad went for the phone, but Mom cut him off before he got there.

A week later, Mrs. Stephens came to our home with a present, a box containing a disgusting new shirt with weird designs on it—I would never wear in a million years. She had stuffed two one-dollar bills in the pocket. I thanked her, pocketed the money, and shoved the shirt in the clothes Mom had been collecting for the church's upcoming rummage sale.

I still repair our neighbors' TV's but make sure there're no dogs present. Oh, the shirt. Mom brought it up to Hilltop Church, along with a lot of other items, for the rummage sale.

Two weeks later, when the sale was over, Mom asked if I would go to the church and help bag stuff that didn't sell, to be given to the Salvation Army. I'm working my way through the piles of clothes stuffing them into bags when I find my awful shirt. *I hope one of those army guys don't wear this, it makes one heck of a target in battle.* I held it up and got Mom's attention. "Mom, see, nobody wanted this shirt either!"

I never made the transition into a career as a TV repairman, but continued to repair TV's and everything else all my life.

Chapter 20

My First Real Job

Mendham Borough, NJ 1956

Growing up in Mendham was great. Being in a small town, everyone knew one another and helped one another when the need arose. Kids enjoyed country living, exploring the woods, playing in streams and swimming in the town's pond. Our telephone provider was New Jersey Bell Telephone. The town population was so small and remote that residents only had party-line telephone service. That meant that you shared a telephone line with maybe as many as six other families. If you wanted to use the phone, you had to pick up the handset to get an operator to connect you. Frequently, you would hear someone jabbering away on the phone. The party-line should have been called a rumor mill generator. Trashy news of all sorts traveled throughout town, courtesy of New Jersey Bell.

It was an absolute shock to my parents when my mother found out she was pregnant in her mid-forties with me. As I got older, I worried myself silly, that my dad might die because he was much older than my friends' dads. He had heart issues and there was little that could be done, except for available drugs at that time. So, when work needed to be done around the yard, I jumped in and did it. *I don't want my dad to die,* went through my mind every day.

Cutting grass was a major chore for the two homes on the property. At an early age of nine, I began to cut acres of lawn with a Bolens walk-behind tractor. I would start cutting one area on a Monday and then progress through other areas in the next few days. When I finally completed the lawns, it would only be two or three days later when I would need to start cutting again. My weekly allowance was thirty-five cents.

I was in seventh grade when the telephone rang; my mother picked-up the call. It was for me. *Who would want to call me?* Remember, I had my own independent telephone system wired to my buddies' home. "It's Mr. Wilson from the church," Mom said.

"Hello, this is Greg," I said.

"Greg, my name is Fred Wilson, deacon of buildings and grounds, at Hilltop Church. We have a need for someone to cut the cemetery grass. Would you be interested in doing that? We'll supply the mower, reimburse you for the gas, and pay you $3.75 per hour."

"Sure! I'd love to have that job. I cut all of my parent's grass, so I have lots of experience."

"Well, you're the first one we thought of to do the job."

"This sounds great, Mr. Wilson. When do I start?"

"How about coming over to the church, around eight o'clock Saturday morning? I'll show you where the lawnmower and gas are kept."

"I'll be there Saturday."

Saturday morning rolled around and I got on my J. C. Higgins bicycle and headed for Hilltop church. I was really excited about the opportunity. *Wow, that would give me lots of money for my projects and experiments,* I realized as I pedaled. The church was a little over a mile away. I reached the center of town and made a left onto Hilltop Road. I saw the church about a quarter of a mile ahead up on top of the hill. I had to pedal harder to get up the hill. Finally, I reached the cemetery driveway, then turned to get to the back of the church building. There was Mr. Wilson, waiting for me.

"Hi, Mr. Wilson."

"Hi, Greg. Let me walk you through what needs to done."

Mr. Wilson walked around the church and showed me areas that needed to be maintained. He pointed to several small monuments that stood only an inch or two above the ground.

"You have to keep your eyes open for these, if you hit one, it will damage the mower blades and ruin the mower."

"Okay."

144

"Here is the key to unlock the tool storage door, I'll open it."

He opened a small rickety wooden door; it was only about five feet high. It was dark inside and smelled damp and musty. *A good place for ghosts to hide during the day* went through my mind.

"There's the lawnmower, and over there's the gas can," he said.

"When do you want me to start?"

"You can start this morning if you like. Give me a call next Saturday and give me the number of hours you worked and I'll mail you your paycheck. Do you have any questions?"

"No sir, Mr. Wilson."

It was about eight-thirty when Mr. Wilson left. I went into the spooky storage area, pulled out the old reel mower, and went back for the gas can. After I filled the tank, I started the mower and headed out to cut the grass. The machine cut well, grass flew out the back all over my Ked sneakers. I concentrated on cutting as close as possible to the gravestones, reading the name of each person buried six feet below. It didn't take much these days to get me spooked considering we had a red barn inhabited by a bunch of unsettled spirits and ghosts.

I worked my way down the hill, cutting horizontally across the line of graves. It was easier to do than cutting up and down the hill. Down at the bottom of the hill were the newer graves. I saw the names of older members of the church who used to worship on Sunday mornings. I remembered most of them. They always shook my hand as I stood next to my parents. Up ahead was a fresh grave, just barren dirt, no grass yet—it creeped me out. The dirt was piled high over the grave to make sure that whoever was buried down there, stayed down there. It made me nervous thinking about a new body lying in a box six feet below. Sweat started to drip down my face as I continued to mow, and the sun beat down on me now. *I wished I had brought water with me, got to remember to do that next time.* Glancing down at my watch, it was almost noon, I should have been starving, but cutting grass for the dead killed my appetite.

I headed up the hill, perspiring like mad, my shirt wringing wet. At the back of the church, I locked-up the mower, jumped on my bike and headed down the road for home. The breeze felt wonderfully cool as it hit my face. It cooled me instantly as I coasted down Hilltop Road. I made the right hand turn onto Main Street and pedaled home.

After lunch, I grabbed a container of water and headed back to the church. As I bicycled to the back of the church, I looked at the large area of grass that I cut—it looked great, neatly cut.

It was one-thirty on my watch when I unlocked the door and got the mower out to cut the grass on the other side of the church. That's where all the really old grave sites were located. These gravestones were made from red sandstone; you could hardly read the names and dates. Some of the stones had sections that had flaked off, while black stains streamed down like tears on the stone's face. Some of the graves belonged to soldiers who had died in battle during the Civil War. I worked my way across the hill, back and forth, glancing down at my watch, mentally adding $3.75 for each hour that had gone by. Once-in-a-while, someone would drive into the cemetery to place flowers at a grave or pay respect to a loved one. It really gave me some company to have a living person in the cemetery. It felt creepy for me sometimes to be the only one living among the dead.

I continued to cut grass at Hilltop Cemetery through May and June. I thought, *what could I do to survive the summer heat?* An idea came to mind, *I must start early in the morning, quit during the mid-day sweltering heat and go back and cut the rest after an early dinner*

It was weird to bicycle in the dark. I had bought a bicycle light at Sears and had mounted it on the handlebar.

On my way to the cemetery in the pitch-black morning, my light had lit up raccoons, rabbits, and deer on my way to the church.

Arriving at Hilltop, I pointed my bike light at the storage door. I removed the key held by a string around my neck, unlocked the storage door, and gassed-up the mower. There were a few homes near the cemetery that would soon be

146

unhappily awakened by the noisy machine. The sun had not come up yet, so it required me to strain my eyes to prevent me from running into a monument. After working my way down the hill, the sun started to appear over the horizon. At nine, I was exhausted and hot. I headed up the hill to cool off under the big tree near the side of the church to have a long drink of water. After some cooling down, it was back down the hill to cut more grass. I lasted until eleven, then put the mower away and headed for home. When I arrived home, I got as far as the couch in front of the fan and fell asleep.

Other than the brutal summer heat, things were really working out well for me. Every week a paycheck arrived in the mail. Mom or Dad cashed it for me and I hid my stash of bills inside my model sailboat. Not having any time to buy anything, it accumulated to a wad of money.

At the end of August, the days got noticeably shorter and I struggled to complete the grass cutting. I had wanted to spread it out over two days, but I also had Dad's lawns to do. It was the last Saturday in August when Big Ben went off at four-thirty. I did the usual and rode my bicycle in the cool morning air to Hilltop. Halfway there my bicycle light quit. Fortunately, it was a full moon that gave me some light to reach the church. As I got to the storage room at the church, I hesitated to open the padlock. I had no bike light to illuminate the inside. One half of me said go home and come back later, but the other half told me to get the lawns cut while it was cool. I chose the latter, held my breath, and turned the key. Removing the lock and opening the door with caution, I stood ready to bolt. I took a deep breath and stepped inside ready for some ghoulish thing to happen. Nothing happened, just the smell of the earthen air. I brought out the mower and went back in for the gas—no luck finding it. I went down on my hands and knees sweeping back and forth with my right hand, going deeper into the storage area. It felt like I was entering a cave. As I went in deeper, my right hand landed on something hard, it felt like a leg bone. *It's a damn femur bone!* I nearly peed myself, as I scrabbled out of the space.

I ran back to my bike, ready to bolt, but tried the light once more—it didn't come on. I gave it a slam with my hand like Dad does to our TV when it's not working right. Like magic,

147

the light came on. *It must have been a bad battery connection.* I rolled the bike up to the open door.

There it was, standing proudly in front of me—a pick-ax. As I studied the oval wood handle, it looked very much like a human femur that I saw on the TV program "*Zacherley.*" In the corner was the gas can, with a note on it. I grabbed the note and brought it up to the light.

"I filled the can for you. You're doing a great job," Mr. Wilson.

After filling the mower, I began cutting grass. It was still dark out. I heard a strange noise, shut off the engine and stood perfectly still. An unsettled feeling of fear grew over me. There was unrest among the dead this morning, for sure.

"Woooooo," sound traveled throughout the graveyard. It was loud and modulated in volume, over ten to fifteen seconds. Probably an owl I told myself. *The mower will scare it away*, I thought. I started the mower and began to cut. The noise began again. I wasn't scaring it away. It was getting closer and louder; it could be heard clearly over the din of the motor. The Woooing was continuous now and at times, sounded like a soul in pain. *Had one of the dead come back to life?*

Frightened, I left the lawnmower running and took off up the steep hill with my heart beating like a machine gun. I struggled to catch my breath to reach the back of the church. I jumped on my bike and pedaled down the hill as fast as I could. When I reached home, I didn't even put the kickstand down, I just dropped the bike. Getting safely inside, I slid the lock bolt home and got under the covers.

Dad always got up early and made breakfast for the family. He went out the back door to bring in the delivered milk sitting on the stoop from Welsh Farms and noticed my bicycle lying on the ground. Knowing that I should be at the church cutting grass, he knocked on my door.

"Greg, are you okay? Don't you feel well? You're supposed to be at the church."

"I'm quitting, Dad! I'm never going back there again, never ever; it's haunted too, dad, just like the red barn!

148

I think they buried someone alive. The stiff somehow dug himself out of the grave and screamed in pain."

"Don't be silly! It probably was just an owl."

"No way! I'm going to call Mr. Wilson later and tell him, I quit."

Glancing over at Little Ben, the dial pointed to eight o'clock. I picked up the black telephone hanging on the kitchen wall and waited until the operator answered.

"Number please," the operator asked.

"I want to speak to Mr. Wilson, right away!"

"Do you have the number?"

"No, can you look it up?"

Moments later, "I'm connecting you now."

"Hello."

"Mr. Wilson?"

"Yes, Greg? Everything alright?"

"No! I quit!"

"You're doing such a great job. Can we work out the problem?"

"Not unless you get the US Army in that graveyard!"

"That sounds extreme."

"Some stiff dug himself out of his grave and scared me half to death. He came after me screaming! I'm never going back there again! I quit! Goodbye Mr. Wilson."

Even decades later, I believe some restless soul wanted me to know I was treading on his turf. As a reader, you might conclude that it was an owl—let me assure you, it was not! As a new member of Hilltop Church, I pass by that cemetery each Sunday and keep a watchful eye on what lurks around the monuments. I'll never set foot in there when it is dark, except on Easter Sunday Ecumenical Sunrise Service when Mendham

149

Protestant pastors are there to drive off whatever unsettled spirit roams in the graveyard.

Chapter 21

Our Skin-Diving Adventure

Barnegat Light, NJ

It was the summer of 1958 and my parents rented a vacation home for the extended season at Barnegat Light. The best part was that our Mendham neighbors, the Larsons, had a summer home there, too. Their sons, Al and Sam, would be there to pal around with me over the entire summer.

There were neat things to do there; fishing, beachcombing, swimming, skin-diving, as well as looking at pretty girls on the beach. I wasn't a great fisherman; standing on the beach, holding a fishing pole, waiting for a fish to take my bait got boring—not my cup of tea. But, diving, that was my mecca. I was greatly inspired by the TV program, 'Sea Hunt,' starring Lloyd Bridges who portrayed a former Navy frogman.

Over the winter months, I saved up my money to buy really good skin-diving equipment—U.S. Divers. In my stash of equipment were the aqua blue colored mask, snorkel, and fins. I also bought a diver's knife and sheath that strapped to my ankle, a spear gun, and an emergency flotation vest. I felt very safe going out in Barnegat Inlet and in the ocean.

Most often I would walk-up to 4th Street, the northernmost tip of Long Beach Island, to access the beach near the lighthouse. Beaches along the inlet were dangerous, especially the one near the lighthouse because of the swift water currents. If you swam out too far, you could be swept into the deep marine channel. I snorkeled a safe distance, parallel to the beach, and drifted at a pretty good clip, getting a great view of everything underwater. The water clarity was spectacular, you could see down twenty feet or more. I never thought about the presence of sharks, which could have been a deadly mistake. There were lots of fish; blowfish, sea robins, striped bass, and sea eels to name a few. Fluke, some so huge they often were referred to as doormats, buried themselves in the sand waiting for their next meal.

Nasty blue-claw crabs were numerous, scurrying around on the bottom. They warned me to stay away from them by raising their claws when I got near. Small sea horses appeared in August when the water temperature was at its warmest. Underwater relics from destroyed homes that got washed away during previous hurricanes lay scattered along the sand, as well as broken china plates, cups, and utensils. You never knew what you would come across from one day to the next, a boat anchor with rope accidentally tossed overboard or maybe an entire fishing pole and reel, each with its own story. Long stretches of seaweed glided back and forth with the tide, loaded with lost fishing lures and tackle. I salvaged expensive Hopkins Luers and pounds of lead sinkers that I sold for spending money.

Riding the fast current took me down to the south rock jetty in about fifteen minutes. As I reached it, the massive boulders and rocks stretched out into the ocean for about a half-mile. There was also a north jetty on the opposite side located at Island Beach State Park. Barnegat inlet flowed between both jetties for all maritime traffic from the Atlantic Ocean. The jetties were marked with port and starboard navigation lights that guided boats safely into the inlet at night.

Fishing boats often came close to both jetties to fish because that's where fish came to feed on mussels and bait fish. The water was very turbulent there during high tide, splashing up over the rocks. Fishing boats that got too close ended up smashing against the rocks. It often happened from an unexpected rogue wave.

Skin-diving off the south jetty was always my dream. I had vivid visions of marine life along the rocks and boat wrecks resting on the sand. But, diving alone without a buddy was a rule you didn't break, so I kept that wish in the back of my head.

My buddies, Al and Sam had an eight-foot pram, along with a small two and a half horsepower outboard motor. They stored the dingy at Myers Yacht Basin, not in a slip like other boats, but turned over upside down on the muddy ground with the anchor set high up in the marsh grass.

One day, my friends and I wanted to take the boat out into the bay to go skin-diving. We got their mom to drive us to the yacht basin, along with the motor and our gear. After we got there, we unloaded the car and thanked their mom. We had to transport all the stuff to the boat. To do that, we had to walk about a hundred feet through seagrass and black colored muck. It stunk, like a combination of dead fish and sewer water. Your feet sank deep into the muck with every step you took, staining your skin. The three of us carried the motor, gas can, two oars, life preservers, and our diving gear to the little eight-foot pram. We turned it over and secured the motor, filled the gas tank, and loaded our stuff onboard. When we finished we looked at the little boat bobbing in the bay. There wasn't much room for us. We were big guys, each close to six feet in height.

We pushed the boat out into foot deep water and steadied it for Al. He ran the outboard. After several pulls, the motor started with a cloud of smoke, billowing out the exhaust near the water. Sam climbed aboard and sat on the middle seat, the boat sank deeper into the water. Jockeying for a place to get in, I almost flipped it on its side. My second attempt, I made it to the front of the pram where there was no seat. My back had to rest on the flat, scow type bow.

Somehow during this awkward process of getting aboard, water got in the boat, soaking our towels that had been placed on the floor.

When the boat stabilized, Al steered it in the direction of the deep channel, about a hundred feet ahead of us. This was the main waterway to get to Barnegat inlet and out to the ocean. We had to circle a few times, to time it right, so that we wouldn't get T-boned by a large fishing boat or yacht. The channel was busy, but our time came to safely cross the channel for the quiet bay. Al turned the throttle to the max for the boat to move at a faster clip across the channel.

We headed for a distant sandbar to beach our boat and snorkel. We suited up with our skin-diving equipment and hit the water. Within a short while, we got bored, nothing really to see—no shells or even a fish, just sand.

"Pretty boring, I didn't even see a fish," Sam said.

"The tide's going out, it would be a good time to go out to the south jetty," I suggested.

"That's pretty dangerous getting around the lighthouse with all those whirlpools and treacherous currents," Al replied.

"Yeah, but if we got around that, we would be home free," Sam said.

"With Al at the helm, we'll make it for sure," I added.

"Just to let you know, once we are in that current, there's no turning back with this small motor," Al said.

"Let's do it," Sam said with a smile on his face.

We got into the pram and pushed it into deeper water with an oar while Al started the engine. We were on our way. In a short time, we reached the channel and it carried us at a fast clip towards the treacherous water around the lighthouse. Our minds were focused on the dangerous water, so focused that we hadn't heard the large fishing boat approaching behind us. Looking back, we suddenly saw the towering hull of the boat. Could he see us sitting low in the water? He started blowing his air horn to get us to move out of the channel. He had a boat filled with anxious fisherman ready to fish. The captain blew the horn again, with a long persistent blast.

"He wants us to get out of his way, Al," I shouted over the noise of the fishing boat and our motor.

"Too bad! As I said before, once we're in this fast water, there's no turning back," he shouted back to me.

As I looked back, the fishing boat was getting closer, trying to bully us to get out of his way.

"This doesn't look good," Sam yelled out.

Seated in the front, I saw a huge bow casting a dark shadow over our little pram. "I hope this guy doesn't ram us," I shouted to Al.

"He's in a maritime pickle. He probably figures if he passes us, his wake would sink us. That would get him a Coast Guard citation and his marine license pulled."

As we approached the lighthouse, the water was getting dark, an ugly green color that indicated very deep water. We heard the fishing boat reverse his propellers to distance himself from us. We found ourselves between, a large fishing boat in the back of us and a huge swirling whirlpool of water in front of us. Tense, we grabbed the sides of the boat and held our breath for what was about to come. The swirling water looked deadly, three times the diameter of our little pram. It snatched us and spun us around.

"Get us out of this death trap! Gun the motor!" I yelled.

"The throttle is at max!" Al shouted back.

The fishing boat behind us revved up its loud diesel engine with a roar. Its reversed props dug in and brought the fishing boat to almost a full stop, providing us a wide birth.

"Al, will you do something!" Sam shouted.

"I'm trying. This motor is useless in this whirlpool current."

Al turned the handle to the right, then to the left. The pram was unstable, rocking from side to side as water splashed into the boat from all directions, sloshing back and forth over the floor as we held on for dear life.

"Grab your life preservers!" Al shouted.

Seeing imminent danger, the first mate on the fishing boat removed the orange lifesaver along with the tethering line and walked to the front of the fishing boat.

"Al! There's a large pleasure boat headed right for us from the opposite direction!" Sam shouted.

The yacht was on course to pass around the lighthouse. They weren't stopping or slowing down, just barreling down on us from the opposite direction. As they got closer, the man and woman looked down at us from the flying bridge and yelled something at us, that we couldn't hear. We then spun around several times when a miracle suddenly happened. The large boat disrupted the spinning whirlpool, just enough for the little motor to take over and let us escape death's grasp. Moments later, we passed out of the treacherous spiral current and headed out into Barnegat inlet.

155

Al steered the little pram for the shallower water near the shoreline. The fishing boat passed us, the captain on the bridge raised his hand with a closed fist, blasting his horn. Fishermen, standing on the side of the boat, gave us a disgusted look. A few placed their hands to their mouths shouting vulgar insults.

Some guy with a Yankee hat yelled, "You're damn lucky to be alive!"

"He's right guys, we are lucky to be alive. God certainly was with us to make it out of there," I responded.

"I'm still shaking," Sam said.

"You guys should have been back here operating the motor—scary as hell!" Al exclaimed.

"Let's get out of the channel into shallow water," Sam said to his brother.

We headed in, towards the beach and calm water for the one-mile jaunt to the south jetty.

It took about twenty minutes to reach the rock jetty, Al made a gentle left turn and motored parallel to the jetty. We got halfway out to the end of the jetty when the water got extremely rough. We feared we'd sink the boat, swung around, and headed back near the beach. After reaching knee-deep water, we threw out the anchor. After the anchor took hold, Sam secured the rope to the middle seat. I jumped out to steady the boat for Sam and Al to get out.

We suited up with our equipment and snorkeled out parallel to the jetty. The current kept forcing us close to the rocks. The jagged broken mussel shells could do a number on us, cutting our skin and flesh like butter. We swam away from the rocks until we got to the choppy mid-point. I removed my snorkel and said, "Let's see what's down here." We all took a deep breath and dove underwater.

On my dive, I got down to about ten feet; the jetty was teaming with fish—huge fish. Large bass passed in front of me, chasing smaller bait fish. My lungs were screaming in pain for oxygen and I came up for air. *Maybe even bigger fish out further*. I swam out north for about a hundred feet and dove down about eight feet—a wreck! The large wooden boat rested on the bottom, split open down the middle. To my amazement, there was a lobster moving slowly around the boat. I dove down deeper to try to grab him. In a flash, he flipped his tail and was gone, leaving a sandy cloud.

Up again to the surface, I trod water and checked to see that my buddies were safe. They were doing fine. I swam out into deeper water and dove again, about ten feet from the rocks. At about six feet down, something caught onto my knife handle and preventing me from using my leg. I bent over and felt what seemed to be a clear monofilament fishing line. I freed the line from my knife and started to surface. As I neared the surface, I got caught in a spider web of several other lines all around me. I struggled to clear them away from me, the air in my lungs nearly depleted, I became light-headed. I needed air! I kicked with all my strength to reach the surface. My left flipper got tangled in the lines and became useless. With my right flipper, I continued to kick like mad, fighting the tension of lines pulling on my left leg.

My head popped up above the surface, I blew the water out of my snorkel and took several breaths. My lungs sucked in oxygen and soon my lightheadedness disappeared. I reached for the knife and started cutting lines. Fishing lines were all over me. Using my hands, I grabbed lines that interfered with me as I inched my way closer to the shore. My buddies were about fifty feet from me. After I got free of the lines, I swam towards them, staying a safe distance from the jetty. When I reached them, I popped the snorkel out and said, "There're fishing lines all along those rocks; it's too dangerous to dive out here. I got caught in a bunch of them—damn near drowned! Two near tragedies in one day, that's it for me. Let's head in," I said.

The three of us were snorkeling in when I spotted the shark swimming below. I tapped Al on the shoulder and pointed to the sand shark. Although he was about four feet long, we were safe. Luckily, sand sharks don't attack humans. Sam dove down to get a closer look and the shark scooted off.

When we got back to the boat, we took turns drinking lemonade from our jug. On our trip out to the jetty, it was at the end of low tide, the slack tide had passed, and now the tide was coming in. We had to get back in during this cycle.

"Let's motor up to the 4th street and beach the boat there. That's not too far from your house," I suggested.

"Sounds good to me. I'm not looking forward to driving this dingy around that lighthouse again. This time we might not be so lucky," agreed Al.

It took us about fifteen minutes to reach the beach. The waves were minimal. Al revved-up the outboard to break through waves, outside the marked off swimming area. He flipped up the motor and we glided to the end of the gentle waves. We pulled the boat up on shore, well past the high tide point. Al, being the strongest of us, unfastened the outboard motor, and placed it over his shoulder underneath a towel for the walk home. Sam and I grabbed everything else.

Later that afternoon, we ran into another friend of ours, Joey. His dad had a Ford pick-up truck. We told him of our exciting skin-diving adventure and our dilemma—our stranded boat sitting on the 4th street public bathing beach.

"Joey, we got to get this boat off the beach, PDQ. Do you think your dad would help us move it to Myers Yacht Basin?" asked Al.

"He's home today, I'm sure he'll help you," Joey said.

Joey split for his house and about twenty minutes later, his dad arrived at the Larson's house with his truck. The three of us piled into the back and we drove down to the end of the street with the flashing amber traffic light.

"Make it quick, there's a no parking sign here," Joe's dad said.

The four of us jumped out of the truck and ran down to the beach to retrieve the boat. We carried the pram up over the dunes. When we reached the last dune, we saw Police Chief Flemming talking to Joe's dad, pointing to the sign. He saw us carrying the boat, and laughed, "It's you guys again! We were friends with the chief and talked to him often.

You guys remind me of the Little Rascals, but older." He got into the police car, shut off his flashing lights, and took off.

The four of us loaded the pram in the back of the truck as Joe's dad grumbled about almost getting a ticket. We apologized for getting him in trouble with the chief as he and Joey got into the truck to drop off the boat at the marina. The three of us began walking up the road to their house.

"Well, that's an adventure we'll never forget," I said with a happy grin.

"Don't ever ask me to pilot that pram around the lighthouse again," Al firmly said.

"Diving off the jetty was terrific—the wreck, the fish!" Sam said with excitement.

"You forgot about the damn shark!" his brother reminded him.

"We should do it again! It was really a cool thing to do. Next time, we can get Joey's dad to drop the pram off at the inlet beach," I suggested.

"Good luck on that!" Al exclaimed.

Chapter 22

Kirsten

Mendham Borough, NJ 1956

I had begun seventh grade when my interests quickly drifted to the opposite sex. I had nothing to do with it, it was their doing. Somehow, my female school friends came back from summer vacation transitioned from classmates to sexy young girls. They reminded me of younger versions of those calendar girls, like the ones that hung up in the repair bay at the Sinclair station across from Gunther Motors, but with more clothes on. Their clothespin-shaped bodies seemed to have transitioned overnight to curvaceous figures, like the Rockettes at Radio City Music Hall. They used to walk like us guys, straight as an arrow, but now, they swayed with a sexy gate from side to side. *They might need wider aisles in our classroom.* Their hair changed too, last June, it just hung down over their heads, but now, some came back looking like movie stars sporting elaborate hairdos.

Annie came back much different too, she's blonde, the prettiest girl in our class. I had to take a second look at her along with her girlfriends. I couldn't believe my eyes. They came back this year with their faces painted! Last year, they only had rosy cheeks once in a while. That used to happen when a girl got nervous or embarrassed, like in class, when the teacher called upon her to answer a question. Now, a few girls looked embarrassed all the time with their rosy cheeks.

There's more, last year their lips were not much different from us guys—we never thought about kissing them. Now, they've painted them with red lipstick to make them stand out, to make you look at them when they give you a sexy smile. They even took time to paint around their eyes, too. They probably did that to make you look their way when they flick their eyelashes and twinkle their eyes at you.

Here is the best part, last year their chests looked as flat as fried eggs under their blouses. This year, the fried eggs grew into navel oranges. Charlie set me straight on those, he's really educated on stuff like that, big time.

"They're called tits," he told me.

"I couldn't believe my ears. What did you call them?"

"Tits."

Being a country boy, I replied, "I thought only cows had them."

"Nope—cows have teats, girls have tits," Charlie said with confidence. Didn't you ever notice grown women?"

"Yeah, the ones in *National Geographic*. One time, Mom slipped and whispered something to another woman about her breasts. Occasionally, Dad whispers, when he sees a pretty lady, but only when Mom's not around, she's stacked! I stored that information in my head." Since he was so knowledgeable, I had to ask another question. "Well, how come some girls have smaller ones, and some have bigger ones?"

"They wear falsies, that makes them bigger and stick out more."

"They wear what?"

"Falsies—fake tits. They're made of rubber or that foamy stuff. In an emergency, if they don't have a pair of falsies, they stuff a pair of socks in their bra," Charlie said.

"Holy crap!" I exclaimed, stunned by this knowledge of the opposite sex. After thinking deeply, I replied, "That's simply incredible....unbelievable—socks for tits!"

After school ended, I headed home thinking about my new knowledge of female anatomy, every step of the way. One thing for sure, socks will have a new meaning every time I put on a pair. As I neared home, I had to get my mind off of tits and planned to do something constructive, visit my best friends. Maybe I'll share my new found knowledge with them. Although, they probably know all about them, being that their mother is a nurse and father is a medical doctor. I changed my clothes and headed across my backyard to their house.

"Al! Sam! You guys there?" I yelled through the screen door.

"Yeah, coming down, Greg," Al replied.

Al arrived at the door and invited me inside. Sam joined us a few minutes later. We sat in the den to chat for a while. I could see Kirsten fiddling around in the kitchen in the next room. I wanted to share my amazing news with my buddies, about what some girls do with their white socks, but Kirsten was within listening distance. I really liked her and didn't want her to get the wrong impression of me. She was a year older and a freshman at Morristown High School. A few minutes later, she came out to say hello and gave chores for Al and Sam to do later that afternoon.

"Hi, Greg," Kirsten said, greeting me with a beautiful smile.

I always thought of her as just Al and Sam's sister, but one look at her today, she looked really special. Kirsten had shed the clothespin image a year or two ago. Other girls in my class turned sexy, but she had turned into a someone special—smart, attractive, and always very nice. She was the most beautiful girl I had ever seen in my life. She had reddish-brown hair that was so long that it went half-way down her back almost to her butt. It flowed like a field of wheat in the wind as she walked. It glimmered as light rays from the window hit it. Her figure was like an hour-glass, like the glass timer in my mom's kitchen. Her body was tan, probably from lifeguarding down at Barnegat Light. Her eyes, they were something else, so beautiful as they sparkled, full of warmth and life. She was gorgeous! So much so, that she didn't have to paint her face in the morning like other girls. Although, she did use red nail polish on her toenails, only the big ones.

My eyes must have been popping out of my head, as I admired her, from head to toe. My parents told me it was impolite to stare at anyone, but I broke that rule everytime time I saw Kirsten. She had an aristocratic demeanor too, like someone of royalty. She had perfect grammar and an extended vocabulary, with an exquisite command of the English language. When you heard her talk, it was like listening to the queen of England giving a speech.

163

Even her mannerisms were like she came from royalty. I often debated in my mind, was she more like a princess or a goddess? She had authority—liked to be in charge, especially of her younger brothers. She had them in total control; do this, do that, and they never argued, they just did it.

As she walked around the room, I wondered if she used socks to make hers point out too. As she walked hers bounced with every step. Being a scientific kid, I figured there were breasts inside her bra and not a pair of socks.

Kirsten had another attribute, not found very often in other people. She was nice, always polite, always liked by everyone. That wasn't just my opinion, but by everyone in our town.

Every time I planned to visit my buddies, my mind was filled with anticipation—would Kirsten be there? Unfortunately, I was disappointed most of the time. She was a popular girl and didn't hang around the house too much. We didn't have any interaction between us, just a hello now and then. However, I did have imaginary conversations with her in my dreams. If I was lucky and got a momentary glance of her, that had to last me days in my head, until I saw her again. Seeing her was like having a pile of gold coins in front of you and you couldn't even take one, you could only look at them.

Golden blonde Annie had long ceased from my nightly dreams—Princess Kirsten took her place every night.

The next summer my parents rented a summer home down in Barnegat Light, the same town as the Larson's summer residence. I must have been a pain in the butt to the Larson's, since I visited them almost every day. Not only to be with my pals, but a chance to see Kirsten. I couldn't believe that she could look any better, but seeing her in a lifeguard's bathing suit was beyond description. If she were in the Miss Universe Contest, she would win, hands down.

Kirsten not only worked as a lifeguard, but also as a waitress in the evening at a local restaurant. I wasn't the only one that knew she was special. She had a string of admirers that pursued her, they saw her beauty too, and her beautiful personality and wanted to desperately date her.

I was unbelievably jealous of them. I would have given anything in the world to have spent just a single minute alone with her.

Gloom and doom came with a double barrel shotgun with the news from my dad. He told me that he had sold the Farmall tractor for four hundred dollars and that we were selling our Mendham estate, moving to a three-bedroom apartment in Morristown. He explained that the upkeep of the property at his age was too much for him. The world came crashing down on me along with all the consequences.

As a young teenager, I cried when a flatbed truck arrived at the red barn the next day to take away the tractor that I had so much fun driving. If that wasn't bad enough, I lay in bed that night thinking that my friendship with Al and Sam would end soon. There was more grief, my lifelong classmates would attend a new school, Mendham Regional High School, and I would be stuck going to Morristown High. But, there was still more bad news, I would never, ever, see Kirsten again. The girl that filled my dreams every night, the girl that made my world a more beautiful place—gone forever.

We moved to Morristown and the first night there, thieves stole all four of my father's expensive wheel covers on his brand new 1958 Edsel Corsair. The following week, someone had climbed the fire escape and tried to break into our apartment through the front door with a skeleton key. As a light sleeper, I heard the guy trying the key and turning the knob back and forth. I screamed, "Help! Robber!" The guy took off down the fire escape in his muddy boots. At that point, Dad had enough, he planned to move at the end of the lease.

A year later, we moved to Morris Plains, NJ. I still missed my Mendham buddies and Kirsten. They were childhood memories that I would always remember. Kirsten had stolen my heart and had a sacred place there. In my mind, she would always remain the perfect woman, a true princess.

Chapter 23

Morristown High School

Mendham Borough, NJ 1956

The summer of 1956 passed swiftly, too fast, as a matter of fact. September had arrived and school would be starting soon. Mendham at that time had no high school and we were a sending district to Morristown High School. Two school buses were used to transport all students to that school. It was clear from day one that there was no late bus schedule. If you missed the bus, it was your tough luck. Mendham's buses were unbelievably old and broke down often, getting us to school late. We were not marked tardy, just jokingly noted as Mendham bus breakdown.

On Sunday evening, the night before school started, my parents sent me packing to bed early. Monday morning, Little Ben, my alarm clock, rang loudly. I stumbled out of bed feeling awful like I never slept a wink. I walked to the bathroom and peeked in the mirror, which confirmed how I felt—crappy. After shaving with my electric razor, I got dressed and went to the kitchen to have breakfast.

"Would you like some shredded wheat for breakfast or something else?" Mom asked.

"Mom! I hate that stuff. That will really make me puke my guts out."

"Probably just nerves. I'll make you some tea and toast."

Fifteen minutes later, I was on my mile-long hike to my old grade school, the bus pick-up point. During my walk, my mind went crazy with what-ifs. What if I got sick, how was I going to get home? What if I can't find my next class in seven minutes? What if I miss my bus?

There was no orientation for our class in the transition from grammar school to high school. In August, I received a mimeographed class schedule along with my homeroom number, 203. By the time I reached the school pick-up point, I was a nervous wreck. My classmate friends, along with the upper-grade classes, were waiting, some huddled like football players planning their next play.

"Hi, guys, ready for the big day?"

"You look like shit, Greg," Alex said, as my friends laughed.

When the guys stopped laughing, I said, "I didn't sleep at all last night. I even tried counting sheep. Besides no sleep, I feel like I'm going to puke.

"Stay the hell away from us! You better throw some cold water on your face when you get to the school," Alex replied.

"I'm really nervous too," Barry said, "My mother signed me up for Latin. She thinks I should study to become a doctor."

"That algebra stuff looks like a killer to me. I have enough trouble adding numbers without adding letters to the mix," Richard added.

Brian was about to add his two cents to the discussion when we saw the two buses coming. Shortly later, they came to a squeaky stop. The first bus filled and my buddies and I headed for the second bus. I worked my way down the rows of vibrating seats holding onto the seatbacks. The engine was running so poorly that it shook the seats like tuning forks. I plopped down in the first empty seat. The rumors were true, these buses were ancient. *Maybe it will break-down and they'll send us home for the day.*

No such luck. Dewey, the bus driver, shifted into first and we were on our way to Morristown High School. The ride over the rolling hills of Mendham Road made me feel worse. Twenty minutes later, Dewey downshifted the bus like a race car as he turned left onto Early Street. Approaching the school, reminded me of a prison, just like the ones I saw on TV. All the lower windows had steel bars. Around the school, hotrods lined the parking spaces, as kids showed-off gunning their cars.

This was so different from grade school, hundreds of kids were loitering around the school, many smoking.

The smoke entered our open windows as we circled to the back of the school. The school was huge and my fears of getting lost in it were confirmed. The school was tall, too, three stories plus a basement where the athletic department was located.

The bus came to a screeching stop and we got out, some sixty or so headed for the double steel doors. With one hand holding my lunch and the other looking at my class schedule, I headed for the nearest stairway, the one in the very front of the building with the wide white marble stairway leading to the second floor.

I went to put my foot on the first step and a kid behind me grabbed me and pulled me back.

"Are you crazy? You don't want to do that," he said.

"Why not?"

"These stairs are only for seniors. By-the-way, I'm Gary."

"Thanks, Gary, my name's Greg—good to meet you. What would happen if I stepped on them?"

"Seniors would have grabbed you and set your ass on a water fountain and you'd be walking around all day with a wet ass."

"Thanks, buddy. So, which stairways should freshman use?"

"All but this one."

I found another set of stairs to the second floor and headed counterclockwise around the entire floor to reach 203 as the eight-AM bell rang. I was dead last to arrive and sat in the empty seat, in front of the teacher.

The teacher looked at me and said, "You just made it." He got out of his chair, scanned the group of kids and wrote his name on the blackboard, Mr. Eckhart. He walked back to his desk and picked up a small Bible. "Each morning we'll start with a Bible reading from the Old Testament, which is acceptable to both Christians and Jews. Then we'll salute the flag. Each month, you'll get a tablet of paper and a pencil.

I'll read your locker numbers off, so copy it down; you'll be sharing it with someone else in the school."

After Mr. Eckhart spoke, the bell rang for the first period, located on the first floor. None of my classes were on the same floor. It was a challenge to reach them before the bell rang. After my last morning class, I headed for the cafeteria. As luck would have it, I took the longest route. When I arrived, the lunchroom was full. I scanned the room and only found one empty seat at a table near one of the many windows. All the tables were eight-footers, solid oak, built to take lots of student abuse. I sat down and said, "Hi, guys."

"Who said you could sit there?" said the big guy in the white tee-shirt with a Camel cigarette pack wrapped up in one sleeve—I never saw cigarettes stored like that before.

I glanced around the table and the guys looked tough, off the street tough, ready to rumble.

"Where are you from?"

"Mendham."

"This is our table is only for the Morristown gang."

"Do you want me to leave?"

"Your choice."

The guy next to me pulled a knife out from his pants pocket and triggered the switchblade open. I looked at the sharp weapon, and swallowed hard. "Next time find another table," he said.

They started grumbling about being in school again and how much they hated it here. Then they started complaining about the awful cafeteria food as I took a bite of my peanut butter sandwich that I had brought from home.

"Tastes like shit," the guy with the cigarettes said, as the others unanimously agreed.

He took his plate with both hands, like he was making a basketball shot, and headed it skyward hitting several ceiling tiles near the next table. Hundreds of kids roared with laughter.

Cafeteria staff tried to investigate, but got caught up having to clean the spaghetti sauce dripping off the ceiling tiles. Several minutes later, the kids went back to their usual loud behavior.

It was a hot day, although the huge screenless eight-foot-high windows were open, they gave little relief from the heat. I went to pick up my sandwich from the table to take another bite, when I noticed that the table had risen a few inches.

"The leg bolts are loose as hell on this shitty table, let's take them off and put them on the floor guys," the cigarette guy said.

Five minutes later, all four legs were on the floor and the table balanced on the guys' knees. I had no idea what they were trying to prove and had lost my appetite for the rest of my lunch.

"Ready guys?" cigarette guy asked.

I sat there and watched helplessly as the table rose slowly, inch by inch, until it got slightly higher than the window sill. One second later, the table was heading down three stories to the driveway below, landing with a loud crash. The cafeteria kids went hysterical, clapping, whistling, and shouting, "Way to go." Then began chanting in unison, "Toss another! Toss another!" Soon, our table-less area fingered us as the guilty party and we were all escorted out of the cafeteria to the administrative office, then forced into a meeting room. The guys were slapping their friends, congratulating one another of their first day's accomplishment. One of the office staff wrote down our names. Mr. La Pointe, the school's principal, came into the room, slammed the door shut, and scolded us for our stupid prank.

He finished by saying, "Someone could have been killed! You're all suspended for two weeks!" and then, he walked back to his office.

"The cigarette guy said, "I told you guys I'd get you out of here for an extended vacation!"

Later, the secretary came in and handed each one of us a pink slip, with big letters on the top, SUSPENDED.

The guys left the room and I sat in the chair, shocked, and bewildered. I got up, went into the office and spoke to a staff member, asking her if I could speak to Mr. La Ponte.

"He's busy in a meeting now."

"I'll wait."

Ten minutes later, Mr. La Pointe's secretary told me he was ready to see me. I was still shaking with disbelief, my first day of high school and suspended for two weeks. What I feared most, was my father's reaction, he would have a tizzy. Aunt Holly would be delighted though, this would support her claim that I was a troubled kid.

I stood in front of the principal's desk to plead my case.

"Mr. La Pointe, I didn't do it. It was the only table that had an empty seat in the entire cafeteria. Honest, I'd never do a stupid thing like that.

He stared at me momentarily and said, "I figured that. You picked the wrong table to sit at. They're all troublemakers, every one of them with juvenile records. Stay away from them! Sorry, this happened to you on your first day here. Give me that pink slip, I'll have the office clear your record."

"Thank you, Mr. La Pointe."

I walked out of his office and glanced up at the clock, 4:10—the buses had left for Mendham a long time ago. I put my hand in my pocket and hoped that there would be a few coins to call home. *I'm stuck here in Morristown.* Panic hit. *How am I going to get home?* I walked up to one of the office staff.

"May I use the office phone to call home?"

"There's a pay phone in the hall for student use," the secretary replied.

"But, I don't have any money."

"That's your problem. We have hundreds of students here and we can't have them use our office phones."

Not having a lock for my shared locker, I walked out of the school carrying my stack of books. *Well, it's either walk or hitch-hike home.* I walked up Early Street, then, headed west on Washington Avenue for Mendham. As I reached Burnham Park, both of my arms were aching from the heavy books. I had never hitch-hiked before, but noticed guys held one arm out, with one thumb up. As cars approached, I shifted my books to one arm and gave the signal—they just zoomed past me. I had walked another half-mile when I tried again, this time a car stopped. The fellow driving looked like an engineer, he wore a Bell Labs ID tag. He was in his forties, thin, dressed in a white shirt and tie. His shirt pocket had a plastic protector filled with pens.

"Where are you going?" He said with a pleasant smile.

"Mendham, Hillcrest Road."

"You look exhausted. First day back at high school? My name is Jerry, what's yours?"

"My name's Greg. Thanks for stopping, I really had a bad day, I even missed my bus."

"Been there, done that. I'll drive you home. Tomorrow will be better, wait and see, Greg. What would you like to be when you finish school?"

"I'd like to be an electrical engineer. I've been experimenting and building electrical stuff for a long while, even an X-ray machine."

"You got to be kidding! That's a mighty dangerous machine, it could kill you."

"My buddies and I never got to test it out. Their dad confiscated it and destroyed it before we even turned it on."

"Well, that was a wise thing he did."

Jerry and I had a great time talking about science. He told me about the transistor that Bell Labs had invented and how it would change the world. He went out of his way and drove me right to my house and dropped me off at my front door.

After I thanked him, I walked in the front door to the family room.

"Where have you been? Dad asked. Your mother and I have been worried sick. She called all your friends, they told her you never got on the bus."

"Suspended for two weeks, Dad. When I pleaded my case, the principal cleared my suspension."

"What! What in the world did you do to be suspended?"

"I sat at a table with some Morristown kids that weren't so nice—they had juvenile records. They tossed the lunch table out the third story window."

"Why would you do a stupid thing like that? Sit at a table with a bunch of hoodlums!"

"I got to the cafeteria late, it was the only place left to sit."

"How did you get home?" Dad asked.

"I hitch-hiked."

"Are you crazy? You don't know what kind of a person might pick you up."

"It's a mighty long walk home, Dad, with four books under my arm."

"Couldn't you call?" Mom asked.

"No money in my pocket."

Dad opened his wallet and peeled off several dollar bills and gave them to me.

"Keep these in your wallet in case you need to call home in the future."

After dinner, I worked on my homework in my room when my eyes closed and I fell fast asleep. I dreamt I was reliving my first day of high school. I was in the cafeteria with those thugs and that damn oak table. They had taken the legs off and had me on the top of the table, heading for the open window. I was heading down three stories, holding onto the table with all my might, and screaming for dear life, inches away from crashing onto the driveway. When I woke up, I turned on my light. Realizing it was just a bad dream, I set the alarm on Little Ben and killed the light. It took me a while to get back to sleep.

Then the second dream started. The thugs had stolen the Mendham bus, they had let everyone go, but me. The hoodlum, with the switchblade, kept opening and closing his knife. The cigarette guy shoved me down on the floor.

With an evil smirk, he said, "You sat at our gang's table, invading our space. We can't have any witnesses, can we, Greg? Switchblade's been dying to try out his new knife. He wants to gut you—gut you like a fish."

Two thugs held me upside down by my legs. I screamed and wiggled trying to get loose. Switchblade stood in front of me, tore off my shirt, and flipped open his knife.

"I got to start higher," he said, bringing the blade closer.

I woke up with my heart pounding and sweat covering me from head to toe. I turned on my light, happy to still be alive. Then, with some apprehension, I wondered what was in store for me the rest of the year. I looked at my calendar and thought, *179 days to go.*

About the stories

Al and Sam Larson were my best friends growing up. Yes, I was completely enamored with their sister, Kirsten—you were and will always be a true princess, Kirsten. The red barn exists to this day; we did make a midnight mission, running back to our homes in terror! I did accidentally go to the wrong church. Murgatroyd did belong to my buddies' parents and we did fight off the German Army on many occasions. We also charged capacitors at Halloween as a trick! We made numerous buggies and did get caught putting my dad's favorite lawnmower gas engine on one—yes, he got very angry!

I know you're dying to know; the three junior scientists, did build an X-ray machine—it was quickly confiscated before we tested it out. The cannon story is mostly true, and the three goofballs did make it over Morris County Police Radio—my dad did get covered with gunpowder. Walter did dig up what he thought was the long sought-after treasure. The twenty-two rifle story happened, thank goodness none of us got hurt.

The Farmall tractor was awesome to drive. Mr. Latterlee, not his real name, was our feared principal and I was forced up the tree one morning, nearly trampled to death by a group of wild horses causing me to be late for school. My dad did teach me how to build crystal radio sets. My buddies had a three-tube experimental kit radio that we enjoyed making pirate radio broadcasts on the standard AM radio band. I secretly recorded family gathering regularly, with my Christmas present, causing family embarrassment sometimes. Annie, not her real name, was a classmate and very attractive and outstandingly nice.

"My First Real Job," did happen and the unknown eerie noise that came out of that graveyard is still a mystery to me. My buddies and I did treacherously go around the Barnegat Lighthouse in an eight-foot pram—my dad, nearly had a heart attack when he found out about it. My little wagon was often seen at Hilltop Church's rummage sales picking up unsold radios. I was the TV repair kid in my neighborhood. I also became a ham radio operator, knocking out my parent's TV and put on 'quiet hours'—thank you, Bob, for the Novice exam.

Acknowledgments

The author wishes to thank Virginia Anderson, retired instructor, County College of Morris, for lighting the spark inside me to write. It is with great pleasure, to have continued our friendship over the years and for always welcoming me to send you stories to read—sometimes returned with gentle corrections and a grade!

I wish to thank Tom Cantillon, Instructor, Union College, for guiding me through each chapter with creative ideas and for editing this manuscript. Many thanks to all the talented Chatham creative writers, they have been nothing less than outstanding, on their suggestions each Tuesday night. To the guy with the red pen—your insight and edits were spot on.

To Carlotta Holton, facilitator of the 'Write Stuff,' Chester, NJ's creative writing group, for the idea of turning my memoirs into a book and her always upbeat spirit and encouragement in my writing—a big thank you. She is an award-winning author of five works of fiction and two non-fiction books.

Also, my thanks to the terrific Chester 'Write Stuff' writers that have listened and laughed as I read my stories to them. Looking forward to publishing our book.

Barbara Henderson and Susan Essock, for making time in their busy schedules, to read, edit, and comment on each chapter—my gratitude and thanks.

Although, not the haunted barn, my thanks to Marie Cogger for permitting me to use a picture of her beautiful barn in Chester, NJ—picture courtesy of Joan Case, photographer.

To Larry Ashley, Ashley Farms, Flanders, NJ for the opportunity to re-live my Farmall tractor adventures by driving his antique Farmall Model C and for permission to use my photograph in this book.

Author's Note

All the stories in this book were based on great memories of my childhood, growing up in Mendham Borough, New Jersey. For the readers' enjoyment, stories have been greatly embellished and creatively written by the author. This book should be considered a work of fiction for entertainment. Any resemblance to actual events and names, living or dead, are accidental. Aunt Holly, my protagonist, was a character of my imagination.

About the Author

Gregory Smith is a retired electronic technologist who worked in new product design, electronic test fixture design, and new product compliance to federal, military, and international standards for the Ohaus Corp. and ASCO Power Technologies. Technical writing began at Gow-Mac Instrument Company writing instruction manuals for all their products. He attended both County College of Morris and National Radio Institute in Washington, D.C. Greg's interest in radio communication began in seventh grade when he became a radio amateur and then near retirement achieved his Advanced Class FCC License of W2GLS. In 2006 he began writing for *Monitoring Times Magazine* with "Tales of a Teenage Radio Amateur," then became a regular writer for the magazine. Three of his stories were chosen as cover stories. "Who Really Invented Morse Code" unveiled the real truth, that Alfred Vail was the real inventor of Morse code. "How to Catch a Spy," kept readers on the edge of their seats as the author and three other radio amateurs triangulated a spy's location in PA, reporting it to the FBI. Years later, CBS broadcasted on *"60 Minutes,"* "The Spy Among Us" believed to be the same spy. The writer is a member of Chester, New Jersey's "The Write Stuff" and Tom Cantillon's Creative Writers' Group in Chatham.